Hearts, Tarts & RASCALS

The Story of Bettys

Copyright © Jonathan Wild, 2005
First published in Great Britain in 2005
by Bettys & Taylors Group,
1 Parliament Street,
Harrogate HG1 2QU

Jonathan Wild asserts the moral right to be identified as the author of this work
in accordance with the Copyrights, Designs & Patents Act, 1988.
Edited by Sarah McKee.
Designed by Georgina Gill and Rebecca Watson.
Printed by Team (Impression) Limited, Leeds.

ISBN 0-9550914-0-3

Contents

Introduction

'Bettys is a rich infusion of past and present which you drink down with your tea, knowing that it is the very essence of Englishness' *Phil Smith – Writer and Broadcaster*

This is the story of Bettys, past and present, from the perspective of the founding family's third generation.

Others would tell it differently, especially my father, Victor Wild, on whose collection of family letters and diaries this book is based. However, it is my hand that is holding the pen, and this is a very personal account, a scrapbook of memories and anecdotes rather than a complete history.

After thirty years working in the family business with the last ten as its leader, I ought to be able to tell you everything about Bettys. That the family cannot in all truth answer the simple question 'Who was Betty?' indicates that some of the gaps between the facts – spaces where true history lies – are not just intriguing, they are downright mystifying. You would expect more precision from a Swiss family; or perhaps, like me, you prefer a good mystery.

My wife Lesley and I in our vegetable garden

For all our Englishness, we are in fact an immigrant family, from that generation of young Swiss hopefuls, like Caesar Ritz, who journeyed, penniless, to the heart of the British Empire in search of fame and fortune. In the course of this story our founder, Fritz Bützer, becomes almost more English than the English. The young 'Fritz' transforms himself into 'Frederick' as he builds his business. Now the successful entrepreneur, he becomes 'Dickie' to his friends. As head of a family dynasty he becomes simply 'Uncle'. *In my heart I am still the same old Fritz'*, he once wrote to my grandmother.

This book is dedicated to my father. He too had his metamorphosis. The young Swiss 'Viktor' had to become the anglicized 'Victor' before he could lead a by now very English business. Seventy years later I think that in his heart he is still that young Swiss 'Viktor'. Try though I might, I have never been able to convince him that a day's walking in the Yorkshire Dales is better than a day in the Swiss Alps.

As for me, I am Yorkshire through and through.

Jonathan

Jonathan Wild
Chairman

CHAPTER 1

The History of Bettys

'So much tragedy all in one night...'

20th December, 1890

It hardly seems fair so close to Christmas: one small Swiss village, Wangen-an-der-Aare, suffering two unrelated family tragedies.

A mother of fourteen children threw herself into the icy waters of the River Aare and drowned; *'the result of a domestic altercation'*, the local paper said. A sad start – or end – to anyone's family history; but it wasn't mine.

That same night, by the same river, the paper reported, a fire broke out at the mill, the home of Johann Bützer, the miller and master-baker. Herr Bützer *'died because of his injuries and excessive inhalation of smoke causing inflammation of the lungs'*. His child, Maria Rosalia, also *'choked in the smoke during the fire, and was buried yesterday'.*

But the paper doesn't tell the whole story: only my family know it.

Amidst the smoke and the flames, Johann Bützer took his five-year-old son, Fritz, by one hand, and his seven-year-old daughter, Ida, by the other. To twelve-year-old Rosalia he shouted: *'Hang on to my night shirt tails!'* Meanwhile his second wife Karolina carried her two babes, one in each arm.

When they emerged safely from the mill, to the father's horror he realized that Rosalia had let go. She was still inside somewhere! Without hesitation he rushed back into the mill and died in vain trying to rescue her.

Two more deaths. *'So much tragedy all in one night'*, the newspaper concluded mournfully with typical Swiss understatement.

This story has been passed down through the family by the surviving daughter, Ida, my grandmother. Her little brother, Fritz, was destined not just to follow in his father's footsteps into the baking trade, but to create one of the most famous tea shops in the world.

For now, though, there was little hope for them. Their natural mother had died of TB three years earlier, so they were orphans.

Ida was taken to live with her stepmother's family. There was no room for Fritz so, as was the custom for orphans with no living relatives or family willing to take them in, he was sent back to the village of his ancestors, Teuffenthal, up in the mountains. There, as was the custom, he was literally auctioned off and 'bought' by a local farmer, who undertook to foster him: feed and clothe him and send him to school. However, the farmer gained not so much a foster child as free slave labour for his farm, for even a five-year-old can work, and won't complain too much if he is half starved and cruelly treated.

There Fritz stayed until he was free to leave on his fourteenth birthday. He was reunited with his sister Ida, completed his schooling, and became a trainee baker.

By 1903 Fritz was qualified. In his exams he scored particularly highly for his dough work but was otherwise signed off as merely capable. He was obviously destined for an unremarkable life in a small baker's

This is the farm-house in Tenffental where FB was foster-boy. Its still the original building as it might have looked to him on his way home from school.

Sketch by
Victor Wild

shop in the Emmental valley. Even the excitement of compulsory military service passed him by. Fit and strong though he was from years of mixing bread dough with the power of his arms and shoulders alone, he failed his army medical because of his poor eyesight.

His imagination and ambition certainly weren't poor. After a childhood of serfdom he was determined now to make something of his life, to be a 'someone', to be his own master. He had intelligence, humour, great charm, and an appreciation of aesthetics and all things beautiful – especially girls! He was naturally inquisitive about the world and hungry to learn.

He wanted to master the arts not just of baking, but confectionery and chocolate, too. He worked his way around Switzerland for three years before moving to Marseilles and then Paris. His sister Ida grew dizzy from so many postcards from so many distant cities!

Paris! What more could an ambitious Swiss village orphan ask for than to be a confectioner in Paris?

No, it still wasn't enough...

The River Aare

The historic covered bridge
by the mill at Wangen

The mill at Wangen-an-der-Aare

The façade survived the fire
and still stands today

Johann Bützer

Miller and master-baker, 1839 – 1890

Fritz Bützer

Happier days before the fire

Albert Ramstein FRIBOURG.

The young confectioner
Fritz, aged 19

Ida Bützer
Fritz's beloved sister

'From distant cities'
Fritz keeps his sister
up to date with his travels

'Maybe I will stay a while...'

12th September, 1907

A letter from Fritz Bützer to his sister Ida, translated from the original German, tells the story of his arrival in Yorkshire.

Meine Liebe Schwester,

Your long expected letter arrived at last. I am much relieved to hear that all is well with you... As for me, you don't need to worry. I've travelled right across France and now across most of England too, with more good luck than calculation! Now I am in Bradford, a town of 450,000 in the north.

The journey was interesting, not to say 'bizarre et amusante...' I left Paris at 8.30 in the evening, after a jolly evening with cousin Adolphe who also gave me a bottle of wine for the journey. On the train I met a young Swiss businessman with his English sweetheart. We embarked at Dieppe, and at one in the morning we steamed off into total darkness and fog. The sea was heaving up and down, but the three of us promenaded on deck, or rather we fell about. But we were in great spirits, and we two Swiss started to sing some traditional songs. This went on until around 3.30am when my Swiss friend went to the railings to 'talk to the fishes'. We made fun of him, but after a while we joined him at the railing. He was so ill he collapsed on to the deck like a dishcloth. When the ticket collector came, I had to go through his pockets to find the documents.

By the time we reached England at 6am I could hardly stand either, and we three had the greatest difficulty in walking down the gangway, clutching each other desperately. In the train we fell fast asleep, and had to be rudely woken up by the conductor when we reached London.

My friends said goodbye, and I was left standing at the platform, suddenly realizing that I had no idea where to find my train and what I had to do with all my luggage. What's more I had lost the address where I was meant to be going. There was a job – with whom? – waiting for me in a town – what town? All I could remember was that the name was something like 'Bratwurst'!

So there I was, not knowing a word of English, not even yes and no. I accosted everyone who came within reach, first in French and then in German, but all I got was blank looks. None of these idiots could speak anything but English!! Finally a little old man offered to help with the few words of French he knew. If I wanted the train to Bratwurst I was not only on the wrong platform but in

the wrong station. He escorted me to a cab, said something to the cabbie, and off I went I know not where.

My rescuer had told me it was Bradford I wanted, which seemed about right but I wasn't sure. Anyway I shouted 'Bratfort, Bratfort!' at any official I could see, and in the end I was shown a train. I even managed to consign my big trunk, which was just as well because when I got off at the second stop to change trains (which is what I thought I had been told to do) the official in whose ear I shouted Bratfort several times looked at me as though I was mad and pointed at the train I had just got off. 'Thunder and Devil,' I thought, I must get back on, which was difficult because it was already moving off.

Anyway I finally reached Bradford – in a sorry state you can imagine – and after a night in the waiting room I went to look round. I found a confectionery business called Bonnet (which was not the name that I couldn't remember) but which was owned by a Swiss, and he gave me a job! I get paid 120 francs per month with free accommodation.

Maybe I will stay a while, but if I can find work in an English business I will get twice as much and that's the main thing... I remain your loving brother,

Fritz

Twenty-two-year-old Fritz Bützer did *'stay a while'* in Bradford, and then moved around from town to town in Yorkshire. His ambition was to forgo the artisan craft of bread and concentrate on the more aristocratic artistry of the chocolatier. He styled himself as *'Frederick Belmont, Chocolate Specialist'*, using the French version of his name, which he thought rather more sophisticated to the English ear.

His reputation must have spread, because in 1912 he was invited to Harrogate by Farrah's – the Harrogate Toffee people – to show them how to make smart continental chocolates.

*Fritz and Claire
courting on the River Nidd*

Harrogate at the time was the classiest spa in Europe, so classy that even the patron of its cricket club was none other than Her Imperial Highness, The Grand Duchess George of Russia.

Fritz looked for lodgings. He knocked on a door in St Mary's Avenue. It was opened by a petite young beauty. Hearts fluttered. He had fallen in love with Claire, his new landlady's daughter.

The boat from Dieppe

Not always such a calm crossing!

The London train

On the right tracks, for the moment!

The train to 'Bratfort'

Illustration by Paul Slater, commissioned by *The Times*, March 2003

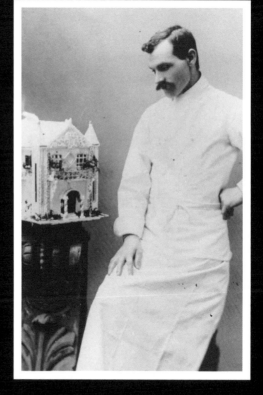

Bonnets Chocolatiers

Fritz's first job in England, 1907

Healthy and chic

Harrogate thrived as the premier
British health resort well into
the 1930s

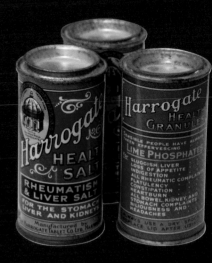

Harrogate Health Salts

They came to take the waters,
would they prefer afternoon tea?

'If I had failed you would never have heard about it'

14th February, 1921

A letter from Fritz Bützer to his sister Ida, after an inexplicable silence of four years. Translated from the original German.

Meine Liebe Schwester,

At last I am able to write a few lines to you. First, my dear sister, please forgive me that I haven't written sooner. I have received your letters and the photographs of your children. My wife is quite jealous over them, especially the younger one. We have no children as yet. I am longing to see you again and I am glad that you are well and happy.

'Fritz Bützer' anglicize into 'Frederick Belmont' by 1921

You will perhaps be curious to know what has happened to your 'dear' brother. Well, he is still the same dear old Fritz. He hasn't changed (my wife says the opposite) – anyway it's hardly surprising that one changes when the world spins round so fast.

During the war I was working here in Harrogate and I became an English citizen and changed my name to Belmont. 'In my heart I am still the same old Bützer.' As an Englishman I was duty bound to join the army and I was called up in November 1918. Luckily the armistice came and that was the end of my war fever. During this time I was able to save some money and in the spring of 1919 I founded a company. Now began a time of my life which I won't easily forget. You will understand what I mean when you read on.

'Muted pink panels' in Bettys Café

Menu illustration, 1930

Well, as I said, I formed a private company with a capital of £5,000 to found a first-class confiserie and café. My own share is one-quarter. A property was bought for £7,000. A mortgage was arranged and then came the equipping.

I must say here that I am the only shareholder who understands the business; the organizing was totally on my shoulders. You can imagine what an effort it was to start such an exclusive business when the whole country was in a state of chaos after the world war.

Opening day was 17th July, 1919, and now came a time of 'either or', 'sink or swim'. Here I now had a shop exquisitely fitted out, the showcases in precious wood, mirrors and glass on the walls, the café furnished in grey, with muted pink panels with old-silver borders,

with old-silver electric candleholders in the centres. On the second floor is a beautifully furnished Smoking Room. The china is grey-blue (white inside), the coffee and teapots in heavy nickel silver.

You can imagine what it all cost, and on top of that all the staff were new. Anyway, we opened, and the first day's takings were £30. After the first week I was sure of our success. Takings were £220. But I had my hands full. Not only did I have to supervise the production rooms on the third floor, but I also had to do the buying. At that time I had about twenty staff.

Quite soon the space turned out to be too small and three months after the opening I looked around for more territory: the second building was opened on 1st August, 1920. Our turnover for 1920 was £17,000. You can imagine how I have my hands full. I am sending you some photos to show you how it looks.

Harrogate is a spa of the first order, and during the summer we had many well-known visitors as customers, for example, Lady Haigh, Admiral Jellicoe, the Duke of Athlone, Princess Victoria (sister of King George V) etc.

Now my dear sister, you know what I have been doing and it's time I drew this long letter to a close. But I must say that I am very proud of my success. Yes, Ida, your brother has gambled and won, and you too shall have your share. Sometimes I wonder whether I wake or sleep. I couldn't bring myself to write to you during the critical time, and if I had failed you would never have heard about it. I only wish our mother was still alive.

I am sending you a photograph of us both taken at our wedding. And a photo of my wife. You can see she hasn't changed. Unfortunately she was very ill in March last year and had two operations. Now she is quite better. It was a difficult and expensive time for me. I am very happy. What I have I owe to my wife. She is not only my wife but my help and colleague.

Please remember me to all our relatives and friends. Your dear letters make me long for home and I shall come to Switzerland as soon as possible with my wife who longs to meet you.

Now I must close, my hand is heavy and I find it difficult to express myself fluently in my mother tongue.

Many greetings and kisses,

F Belmont

The shop was 'exquisitely fitted out'

Menu illustration, 1930

15

Opening day

The original Bettys Café, Harrogate, 1919

Another dream accomplished

Bettys Bakery opens, 1922

The new confectionery room

"LADY BETTY"
Peppermint
Creams

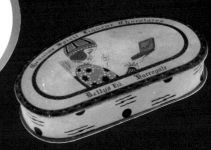

Bettys chocolate boxes

1920s

Man about town!

On the piste

Frederick and Claire Belmont

'Marvellous experience, but costly as usual...'

27th May, 1936

It was the society event of the year, if not the decade. On its maiden voyage from Southampton to New York, the great Cunarder, the *Queen Mary*, was packed with the great and the good. The first-class passenger list sparkled with stars from both sides of the Atlantic. The *Daily Sketch* recorded the sophisticated scene in the first-class dining saloon. Right in the centre of the photograph are Fritz Bützer and his wife Claire. The Swiss foster child and his bride, now known to their friends as 'Dickie' and 'Bunny' Belmont, are mixing with the glitterati!

Dickie's new-fangled cine camera, bought especially for the trip, records glimpse after glimpse of the ankles, calves – and just a little more – of the leggy blonde starlets playing deck quoits.

A stroll around the promenade deck, a quarter of a mile, takes fifteen minutes, plus stoppage time to film a smile and a thigh or two. The Olympic runner, Lord Burghley, runs a lap of honour in full evening dress in less than sixty seconds, but these promenaders take it slow. They have to see and be seen, to film and be filmed.

It's a gruelling dining regime: breakfast at 8 or 9am; soup on deck at 11; lunch at 12.15 or 1.30; afternoon tea at 4; and dinner at 6.30 or 7.45.

A scene out in the Atlantic – in the magnificent first-class saloon of the Queen Mary.

Caught by the Daily Sketch, *29th May, 1936*

Looking at the *Daily Sketch* photograph, perhaps Dickie is suggesting an after-dinner visit to the card tables. He loves a flutter. Bunny reaches into her handbag for the ship's information booklet and sternly reminds Dickie that *'professional gamblers are reported as frequently travelling in Atlantic ships and passengers are warned to take precautions accordingly'.* So, he probably settles for a whisky and a cigar in a comfy sofa, and they reflect on their good fortune. 'This is the life, eh?'

The maiden voyage of the *Queen Mary* really was their extravagant trip of a lifetime. Dickie and Bunny wanted it to last forever. Of course they bought mementoes of the voyage for themselves, and little sailor dolls for the daughters of their friends; but they were cooking up an even more elaborate scheme to perpetuate the voyage. In his diary entry for 6th March, 1937, Dickie writes: *'Nearly another year since my last entry. Lots of things have happened since. First maiden voyage with* Queen Mary *to New York. Marvellous experience but very costly as usual. Further I acquired premises in York, excellent site, best in York for £25,750.'*

Now they would build their own *Queen Mary*! The liner's interior designers and shopfitters were hired. No expense was spared: walnut pillars and panelling, etched glass, exquisite marquetry... just like the great Cunarder: it was madness!

In 1999, eighty-three-year-old Harold Clark wrote to me of his *'many happy memories'* as an apprentice joiner working on Bettys York.
'I was loaned to Messrs Trollope & Colls, a London firm, whose tradesmen came down from Glasgow, where they had been fixing the panelling on the liner the Queen Mary, *and Bettys panelling was to be the same.*

'Mr Belmont visited the premises every week and he was very kind always to leave a five pound note. My share was 10/- which was a lot of money when I was earning less than 20/- a week. When Mrs Belmont came she always kindly gave me a £1 note.

'I have had a wonderful working life with many memories, but none so dear as the time I worked at the new Bettys café in York and the great kindness of Mr & Mrs Belmont.'

CUNARD WHITE STAR
TO NEW YORK

This is the life...
Dickie Belmont with his cine camera

At home on the ocean waves
Dickie and Bunny Belmont

The sailor doll
A souvenir from the voyage

Relaxing on the sun deck
First-class sunshine

Deck quoits
'Ankles, calves, and just a little bit more!'

Cunard White Star

First there was the Queen Mary...

OBSERVATION LOUNGE & COCKTAIL BAR   R.M.S. "QUEEN MARY"   FIRST CLASS

GRILL   R.M.S. "QUEEN MARY"   VERANDAH

RESTAURANT   R.M.S. "QUEEN MARY"   FIRST CLASS

...And then there was Bettys York!

Bettys Ballroom

Bettys Belmont Room
with its exquisite marquetry

The Queen Mary
teapot

Dickie's diary, 16th June, 1937: *'We had a great opening at York on June 1st. Lord Middleton performed the opening. We had a good send off. At the same time I still regret that we took York. It will be a great worry and responsibility. I was wonderfully situated financially and I reprove myself daily for opening York. I do not anticipate great returns, well it is done now and so I must carry on and make the best of it. Bunny has been a little brick. She helped me marvellously. She has any amount of pluck.'*

It has been eighteen years since they opened their first tea room in Harrogate. A purpose-built bakery followed in 1922; then a tea room in Bradford in 1924. This latter venture was a great delight to Dickie; for the premises he took over were none other than those of Bonnets, his first employers in 1907. Leeds followed in 1930. His diary entry for 28th March, 1931 records: *'Well it is done. Leeds is proving a great success. We opened with a great noise and in good style. It is really gratifying to have accomplished my ambitions.'*

This was a rare note of optimism. The reality was that Bettys was not a gold mine. Dickie always, always wanted his cafés 'just so', and would invest lavishly even when the company didn't have the money.

Diary entry for 4th August, 1930: *'Anticipate Leeds expenses to be £6,500 in all. I have only £1,500 so far.'* 2nd October, 1930: *'Seen bank managers, things are a little critical financially. Well anything worth having is worth fighting for.'* 28th March, 1931: *'Leeds has proved much more costly; I think we have spent £8,500.'*

Things improved significantly for Bettys early in 1936 when Dickie sold the freeholds to the Harrogate and Leeds properties and leased them back. Even so, a few months after the *Queen Mary* voyage he recorded that *'the financial position is still rather tight but I think by persevering we will be able to manage'.*

1929

We Invite You

As for his personal finances, they were even worse! Whatever capital he did save he used to buy Bettys shares from the investors who had put up the original capital to start the business. The diary entries for the 1930s are peppered with assessments of his personal finances: *'Unsatisfactory. I wonder when it will improve'*; *'Actually entered a newspaper Derby competition with a view to make money. I could do with £200 to settle everything up. Don't know what to do'*; *'still unsatisfactory'*, *'still bad'*, *'still very poor'*, and a few months after the *Queen Mary* voyage: *'My affairs are still not too good but might and could be worse! I am thinking of flying to Switzerland to see my sister and the children. I do not yet know if I shall go or not. We went for a staff trip, 120 of them... well I am proud of them and of my firm.'*

Adverts commissioned from T. J. Bond, a well-known illustrator of the era

"We shall not be in for lunch Mary — we will lunch at Betty's"

An excellent lunch for discriminating people.   Good food, well served.

Four Course Lunch 2/-
or A La Carte.

HARROGATE   -   LEEDS   -   BRADFORD.

1933

"Yes, darling, you may go to that party. I know they get all their things from Betty's."

Goods from Betty's are always of the finest quality, distinctive and reliable.

SHOP AT BETTY'S—THE HOUSE OF QUALITY.

Betty's Ltd Confectioners & Caterers,

CAMBRIDGE CRESCENT - HARROGATE.

1936

Bradford, 1924

The second Bettys included the 'Mayfair' function rooms

Leeds, 1930

The third Bettys at the corner of
Commercial Street and Lands Lane

STAFF OUTING WINDERMERE

York, 1937

The official opening of the fourth Bettys, 1st June, 1937

BETTY'S STAFF TRIP.

MOTOR TOUR TO THE LAKE DISTRICT.

Five chars-a-bancs accommodating about 120 employees of Betty's Ltd. from Starbeck, Leeds, Bradford, and Harrogate, started at 7-30 a.m. on Sunday for a motor tour to the Lake District. Breakfast was served in the country about two hours later, and after a short stay at Ambleside a stop was made at Keswick for lunch. At 4-30 the return journey was begun.

The trip was favoured with exceptionally fine weather. After an early mist and some rain the sky became almost cloudless. The route lay through beautiful country, and the drive was greatly appreciated.

At 8-30 supper was served at Hellifield. Replying to a vote of thanks from the staff, Mr. F. Belmont (chairman and managing director) said the directors appreciated the close co-operation and harmony that existed between the management and the staff, and that each employee was individually responsible for the success of the firm, and it was gratifying to know that in spite of difficult times the number of employees had reached 142.

After a hearty sing-song a sunburnt happy crowd made for home.

Harrogate Advertiser, 1931

'It is like a fairy story'

2nd October, 1952

It was a sunny Saturday morning. He may have been sixty-seven years old but Dickie Belmont still enjoyed the company of a lady, especially a Swiss one! Whilst the public thronged the cafés on the ground and first floors of his Harrogate premises, in his second-floor office Dickie was having a very private cup of coffee with his great friend Wanda. A Swiss émigré like himself, Wanda too was now anglicized, and they spoke together in English. No one overheard their conversation, so we have to imagine him reflecting on his good fortune and many mishaps over the last fifteen years. 'This is the life!' he would have said, but there would have been sadness in his voice. Everything had not gone his way.

True, business had prospered, especially at York. A full publican licence had been obtained for York *'for the paltry sum of £1,000 from Sir William Foster Todd'*, his diary records. *'What a stroke of luck. It is like a fairy story. Our balance sheet shows profit for York £5,000 and £14,000 for the company.'*

Then there was war. Food shortages and staff shortages brought the business to its knees, in spite of the insatiable demand from the public. The Canadian bomber pilots who were based at a dozen or more airfields around York made Bettys Bar in York their home. Five hundred of them scratched their names on a mirror behind the bar with a diamond ring. Many of these airmen died, many were decorated, many returned years later with their families to show them their signatures.

The basement bar at Bettys (now the Oakroom) was known as 'The Dive'. The reputation of the Canadian airmen for charm, good looks, and deep pockets spread around Yorkshire, and at weekends chars-a-bancs of girls from Leeds would descend on the 'Dive' along with the local talent. It was a bittersweet party time.

Busy though Bettys York was in wartime, the authorities twice proposed to requisition it for official use. Dickie Belmont smiled at the memory of his ripostes, both times so short and sharp that the authorities relented, realizing that to close Bettys was unthinkable.

An incendiary bomb crashing through the roof nearly did close Bettys York, though. Tom the van man was the duty firewatcher that night, and bravely put the fire out before it could take hold.

Around the rest of the Bettys branches, Dickie recalled, the challenge was to concoct meals out of powdered egg, fish scraps, grey 'utility' flour, and the more exotic supplies sent over from America: corned beef, tinned spaghetti, and beans. Restaurants were not permitted to charge more than five shillings for a three-course meal.

Bettys were better than most at eking out their supplies and always had the largest queues in town. Once, Dickie bought a lorry-load of burnt and sooty honey salvaged from a burnt-out London warehouse. He turned it into fudge, a delicacy – like all sweet things – so rare that people queued down the street for a small piece.

Catering for wartime weddings was a nightmare. On more than one occasion the bride had to make do with a fully iced cardboard box instead of a cake. Whatever the improvisation, the brides were invariably grateful.

By the end of the war Dickie's morale was so low and the company's finances so poor that he actually sold Bettys York to North British Hotels. In fact he felt like selling out altogether. It wasn't as if he had a family to share his business with. Only pride in his beloved creation kept him going.

'We have no children yet,' Dickie had written to his sister in 1921. Dickie and Bunny never did have any children. At the age of 51 Dickie, anxious for an heir to take on his business, asked his sister Ida in Switzerland if he could have one of her three teenagers to bring up as his own.

Dickie and Bunny visit Ida in Switzerland, 1930

Ida was struggling to make ends meet as her husband, Carl Conrad Wild, spent most of his income from his accounting job at St Gallen town hall publishing his philosophical writings at his own expense and hiring halls to give public speeches on world peace. He was horrified at mankind's inability to create a better world, and was determined to make a difference personally.

Carl Conrad Wild

At one stage he gave up his clerical job to set up a business bringing sweetness and light to his fellow countrymen. Reading how ancient civilizations believed in the special powers of honey, he decided he would reinvigorate the Swiss people by selling them honey by the spoonful, daily, door-to-door. The young sales girls who he employed were instructed to seal each sticky transaction with a kiss. The venture was not a success. No wonder his family were impoverished.

7TH PARA BATT
REG COULTAS
5TH PARA BRIGADE
KEN. RUDDY
6 OCT. 1943

61 SQ 77'
RCAF W. Quigley

The Dive

Bettys infamous bar and a selection of signatures from the wartime mirror

"WING DING"
Sgt. Brullinger

JN Fletcher
R.C.A.F.
VANCOUVER, BC
CANADA

J E McDonald
420 RCAF
1-2-45

SL McCulloch
R C57311 RCAF
H IH

The requisition letters

REF.NO:5QC/21.

1 Queens Road,
HARROGATE.

11th August, 1943.

The Secretary,
Messrs Betty's Ltd.,
8/11 Cambridge Crescent,
Harrogate.

SUBJECT: BETTY'S CAFE, DAVYGATE, YORK.

Dear Sirs,

With reference to your premises in Davygate, York, I should be glad if you would let me know what your reactions would be if the whole of your premises mentioned above were requisitioned.

Would you please also inform me what you would expect in the way of compensation rental.

Yours faithfully,

J Manson Capt

Lieut-Colonel,
Quartering Commandant, No. 5 Area.

12th August, 1943

Dear Sir,

We acknowledge receipt of your letter dated 11th August with very great concern. We must point out that we serve an average of 20,000 (twenty thousand) Main meals, Subsidiary meals, Teas and Hot beverages, per week. In addition we are retailers of bread and flour confectionery. The Bars are also popular and are largely patronised by the forces.

We maintain that we perform an essential public service in York and we sincerely hope that you will not find it necessary to commandeer the establishment.

We trust to be favoured with an interview at your convenience.

Yours faithfully,
BETTY'S (HARROGATE) LTD.,

Chairman and Managing Director.

Lieut. Colonel,
Quartering Command No. 5 Area,
1, Queen's Road,
Harrogate.

"Here's Betty's Bar"

A popular wartime haunt

Bettys Bar was so famous that it even featured in a cartoon in *The Tatler*

...and only thirty minutes 'til closing time!

Canadian airmen would do anything to get to Bettys Bar!

A FULL SCALE A.R.P. TEST, the first of its kind, took place in Harrogate on Sunday.

The Bettys ambulance

Once the bread was delivered, Bettys vans help with the war effort, 1940

REF:NO:5QC/21.
JCH/CFCT.

1 Queens Road,
HARROGATE

SUBJECT: BETTY'S CAFE, DAVYGATE, YORK.

13th August, 1943.

The Secretary,
Messrs Betty's Ltd.,
Cambridge Crescent,
Harrogate.

Dear Sirs,

I acknowledge receipt of your letter of the 12th instant, and in view of the contents it is not proposed to continue with the requisitioning of the above named property.

Yours faithfully,

Lieut-Colonel,
Quartering Commandant, No. 5 Area.

JCH/CFCT.

War is over — Smile please!

The ladies of Bettys Harrogate

In March 1936 Ida's thirteen-year-old son, Carl Viktor Wild, volunteered for the English adventure. Like his uncle before him, he arrived speaking not a word of English. He was groomed first as an English gentleman at Sedbergh, the Yorkshire Dales boarding school. In the holidays he worked in the bakery and used his artistic talent to design advertisements for Bettys. Then began his catering training. Never mind the blitz and the doodlebugs, Dickie sent Victor to the best hotel in London, Claridges, to train.

Victor Wild's reconstruction of his original 1943 artwork

While the exiled crowned heads of Europe swanned around in the elegant public rooms and suites of Claridges, Victor spent month after month in the underground kitchens cleaning chickens and gutting fish. To this day he has no idea what the hotel looks like. To keep himself sane, Victor rented an attic room nearby, hired a piano, and passed the time between shifts playing music, drawing, and painting. News of his artistic ability spread to the kitchens at Claridges, a hotbed of communists, and he was asked to design posters for a new hotel workers' union. War or no war, Victor recalls, conditions were abominable.

As soon as the war was over Victor returned to Switzerland, training in hotels and restaurants in Zürich, Pontresina, and his home town of St Gallen.

Dickie Belmont wasn't sure whether Victor would ever come back. Victor had missed his mother sorely – and his sisters – and wasn't overly anxious to come back to a country still beset with shortages and rationing. However, return he did, in 1948, and the much-relieved Dickie became more positive about the future. Victor persuaded him to try and buy Bettys York back, which he did in 1950 for less than he had sold it for in 1947! It was to York, to the biggest Bettys of them all, that Victor was sent as trainee manager.

By 1952 Dickie had more family around him than just Victor. On holiday on the south coast in the summer of 1946, Dickie and Bunny were captivated by a bonny baby on the beach. They determined to adopt her and give her the chance of a better life. So arrived Valerie, a delightful two-year-old.

Fifty-five-year-old Bunny sought out a nurse to help her with this new parenting challenge. So arrived Kay. As is usual in our family, hearts fluttered. Soon Victor married Kay and started a family of his own.

On that sunny Saturday morning of 2nd October, 1952 Kay was pushing their big carriage pram down Otley Road in Harrogate with two-year-old Elizabeth and four-month-old Jonathan on board.

Valerie Belmont, a daughter for Bunny and Dickie

Victor Wild

Learning to be
an English gentleman, 1936

Victor and his fellow chefs

St Gallen, 1945

We have pleasure in announcing

that

BETTY'S CAFE RESTAURANT St. Helen's Sq., York

IS NOW AGAIN UNDER THE FULL CONTROL OF
THE ORIGINAL OWNERS

Betty's Cafes LTD.

HARROGATE

YOU WILL FIND THERE THE SAME HIGH QUALITY FOOD
AND COURTEOUS SERVICE AS IN OUR OTHER ESTABLISHMENTS
AT HARROGATE, LEEDS AND BRADFORD

WE INVITE YOUR PATRONAGE
ON YOUR NEXT VISIT TO YORK

PUTTING IT PAT.

Amazing But True!

38,814 lbs. of Butter have been used by Betty's
during the past 12 months in their various productions.

Our schoolboy artist estimates that if made into
butter pats and placed on top of each other they
would make a column

8¾ MILES HIGH.

ALL Betty's products are made of best butter.
Another reason why the quality of our products is
always reliable and uniform.

Betty's Ltd (HARROGATE)

HARROGATE
LEEDS
BRADFORD
YORK

Jonathan and Elizabeth Wild

Posing for the press, Easter 1953

Kay Wild

New Year's Eve, 1950

Advertisement designed
by schoolboy artist Victor Wild, 1939

Whilst Dickie and Wanda were reminiscing over coffee in Harrogate, in York that same October morning Victor was in the kitchens ensuring everything was ready for a busy lunchtime. He was called to the phone; it was Miss Leggett from the Harrogate office. She told him that Mr Belmont had collapsed in his office. The doctor had been called and was with him, but she feared he had passed away.

Victor drove straight to Harrogate and found his uncle's body laid out on the office floor. There was no way that his body could be carried respectfully down the winding back stairs of the building. He would have to be carried down the front stairs, past the café, and out through the shop. Closing Bettys for the day was unthinkable, so Victor kept a vigil over the body until 5.30pm, when the undertakers arrived to carry Frederick 'Dickie' Belmont away from Bettys, privately and with dignity.

Victor Wild's cartoon of himself, 1948

Twenty years earlier Dickie Belmont had written in his diary:
'I shall point out some remarks about what are the best things in life.
I think the following;
1) Enough money to be independent.
2) The glow you get from giving somebody something, which is far more glowing than the glow you get from receiving something (except a thick ear).
3) Sleep. Really I think this ought to be higher.
4) Landing at any seaport after a rough journey.'

Dickie was an intermittent diarist. Had he ever revised the entry he might have scribbled underneath:
'5) And the best way to end life is to be taken by surprise, surrounded by what one loves best.'

Victor Wild's cartoon of Dickie Belmont, 1948

A sixtieth birthday card drawn by Victor for his uncle

In the fairy stories the frog prince lives happily ever after. Fritz Bützer, the poor Swiss orphan transformed into Frederick 'Dickie' Belmont, English entrepreneur, probably died happily ever after, sitting in Bettys, with the premises full to bursting with customers anxious to have a taste of what he had created, and willing to pay good money for it: What a way to go, eh? What a way to go...

The *Harrogate Herald*, November, 1947

'Best Boss'

'He's the best boss in the world. He's more than a boss, he's a friend,' said Mary. And everyone round her agreed. She was standing, wine glass in hand, on the beautifully carpeted floor, which, twenty-eight years ago, she had scrubbed the night before the 'boss', had opened his business for the first time. Mr F. W. Belmont, founder and proprietor of a Harrogate café, is the 'boss' and Mary, with other departmental heads of the firm, had invited him to his own café on Wednesday evening so that they could present him and Mrs Belmont with his portrait. Mr Belmont, a Swiss, arrived in England forty years ago and made his way to Bradford, arriving completely penniless. He took a job in a confectionery business and quickly decided that he would start his own firm.

The portrait presented to Mr Belmont on Wednesday was painted by Mr John A. Berrie, the eminent artist who recently painted Lord Mountbatten's portrait. Mr Berrie was present on Wednesday's unveiling and received many congratulations from the staff on his execution of their commission.

HE IS TRYING TO MAKE US BELIEVE THAT HE IS ONLY TASTING THE WINES TO SEE IF THEY ARE FIT TO SELL.

But there is one thing about our boss - he is always ready to help —

One of many birthday cards illustrated by Victor Wild

Early days
Staff outing to Whitby, 1921

At home...
His last trip to Switzerland

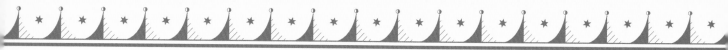

'In the right direction, I hope'

20th July, 1962

A new diary to peep into: my father Victor Wild's. *'C. E. Taylor agreement signed at £180,000. A big step for Bettys! In the right direction, I hope.'*

It had all started with an overheard conversation in Bettys in Harrogate. Naturally, Bettys customers can chatter away about gossip and scandal knowing that Bettys waitresses will hear everything but listen to nothing. They are the soul of discretion. Well, usually; there are exceptions.

In the spring of 1962, the café manager, Miss May Carter, who had served Bettys for over thirty years, excitedly told my father that she had overheard some businessmen talking about the Taylor family putting their business up for sale. Like Bettys, C. E. Taylor and Co. was a Yorkshire tea shop business, but whilst Bettys had a bakery at its heart and soul, Taylors had a little tea and coffee importing, blending, and roasting business.

Victor leapt into action and made an immediate offer at the asking price of £180,000, having secured a large bank loan. Why on earth did he take such a huge risk?

Dickie Belmont's sudden demise in October 1952 nearly led to the death of Bettys. Heavy death duties were payable, and the company almost had to be sold. Victor Wild was thrust into the role of managing director and at twenty-nine years old he felt totally unprepared for the task ahead. Bunny Belmont was the new chairman, but she was already tired and retired.

It took ten hard years for Victor to stabilize Bettys; to deal with the tax issues and rebuild the product range and menu after years of rationing. Victor always says that it was Kay's steady help and support that made all the difference.

As Victor gained in confidence, he wanted to prove himself not just as a steward of his uncle's creation, but as an entrepreneur in his own right. He opened a late-night espresso bar in Street Lane in Leeds, but the 'bike boys' – mods and rockers – proved too hard to handle. He opened a smart Italian restaurant in the basement of Bettys York. He bought a house to accommodate all the Italian chefs and waiters, but their romantic antics proved too hot to handle. He opened a continental delicatessen next to Bettys in Harrogate, which introduced northerners to a whole new world of delicacies that we now take for granted. All these were ahead of their time, anticipating the less conservative, more experimental mood of the 1960s.

Miss May Carter
and the Italian waiters

Is she telling them about the sale of Taylors?

Victor Wild

Takes the helm
at age twenty-nine

The Coffee Shop

Street Lane, Leeds

Bettys Delicatessen

A novelty for
the North

The Oakroom Restaurant

The Italian waiters at Bettys York

Now, in 1962, the purchase of Taylors was Victor's opportunity to prove himself his uncle's worthy successor.

The founder of Taylors, Charles Edward Taylor, was born on 31st July, 1866. His Quaker father, once a pea-dealer, was now a master-grocer in York.

All the Taylor children went to Quaker schools, and it was Quaker connections that landed the two eldest Taylor boys apprenticeships in London with the Ashby family's tea and coffee business. Whilst Llewellyn, the eldest son, was a great success following his training as a tea and coffee taster, Charles Edward struggled. Llewellyn became a sales manager and was later offered a directorship at Ashbys. Young Charles, – and he was still a teenager at the time – was sent to pioneer sales in the south-west. He felt that in this part of the country both the water and the clientele were very different, so he continually asked the Ashbys' buyers to source him teas specially suited for this market. Teas were stockpiled, but young Charles was unable to sell them. He was sacked.

They say failure is not in falling down, but in staying down. Encouraged by his father and elder brother, Charles decided to set up his own tea and coffee business in Yorkshire. Llewellyn became his sleeping partner, providing financial backing and, through Ashbys, buying his tea and coffee at the weekly London auctions.

Charles opened a small warehouse in Park Row in Leeds, but quickly realized that there was too much well-established competition. Instead, he looked to the booming new spa towns of Harrogate and Ilkley, where he opened 'Kiosk' tea and coffee shops with tasting rooms attached where local guest-house proprietors could come and taste his wares and choose blends precisely right for their local water source.

It wasn't long before the tasting rooms became cafés, dark and smoky like the old London coffee houses, where local businessmen met, with runners bringing documents from their offices so they could spend the whole day drinking coffee.

In 1896 Charles ventured further into catering, opening a much more genteel café in Ilkley, the Café Imperial, and in 1905 another Café Imperial in Harrogate in a newly built mock Scottish baronial castle at the top of Parliament Street.

Further Kiosks were opened in Wakefield and Keighley and St Anne's-on-Sea, and Taylors also took over the catering at The Tea House in Harrogate's Valley Gardens, at the Winter Gardens, and at the Royal Spa Concert Rooms. Charles and Llewellyn each had one son, who they groomed for succession, starting like themselves with training with Ashbys in London. The Great War intervened. Llewellyn's son, Bernard, served in the cavalry. He returned safe and sound, but the ghastly experience of the Western Front made him want to live each day to the full, to have a good time rather than take business too seriously. Charles's son, Douglas, lied about his age and joined up at seventeen. He returned within a few weeks with a badly injured hip. Always a timid, languorous lad, Douglas became neurotically insecure. Only strict routines and the minimum of stress kept him sane.

Both brothers served as directors, but, having no children themselves, looked to their wider family for someone to run the business for them. Just as Frederick Belmont found a nephew, my father, to 'adopt' as his successor, so too did the Taylors find a nephew to provide succession.

Bernard's wife, a music-hall star whom he had courted and won at the stage door, had an equally theatrical sister, a Shakespearean actress who was always on tour. As she needed a permanent home for her young son James Raleigh, the Taylors 'adopted' him. When he left school in 1920, he was sent to London to learn the tea and coffee trade at Ashbys before joining the family business. James served the Taylor family loyally and became chairman in 1956.

The Sign
of
Good Service.

James had no children either, so with no succession and a declining business with little profit, the family decided to put the ailing business up for sale, and realize the value of their properties if nothing else.

James stayed on after the takeover by Bettys in 1962, 'just for a few months' to help with the transition and look after the highly specialist job of tea and coffee buyer. In the end, he stayed on another twenty-five years and trained both my brother and me, as well as our present head coffee buyer.

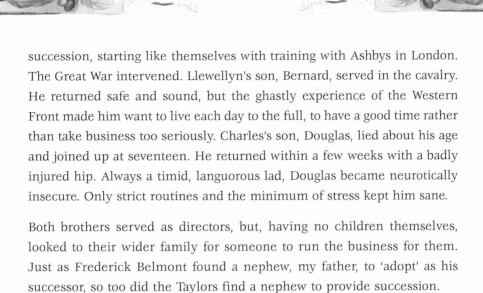

Bettys now owned nine cafés in all, including three in Harrogate. It took more than a decade for Victor and Kay to sort these properties out. Victor decided not to drop the Taylors family name, and all its history with it, but to focus it on its roots, in tea and coffee importing. Bettys would stay as the name for his tea shops and bakery, and the best of the buildings were converted to Bettys. The present Bettys Harrogate is the old Taylors Café Imperial; similarly the present Bettys Ilkley is the former Taylors Kiosk café. Little Bettys in York was also formerly a Kiosk café.

At the end of his diary entry for 20th July, 1962, Victor writes:
'On October 2nd it will be 10 years since Uncle died. Auntie tells me he once nearly accepted a job with C. E. Taylors in 1918.'

This reversal of fortunes is an irony which Dickie Belmont would have loved.

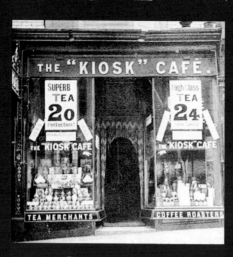

The Kiosk Cafe and Tea and Coffee Stores,

Charles Taylor
1866 – 1942

The first Taylors Kiosk
16 Parliament Street, Harrogate

Llewellyn Taylor
1861 – 1935

VALLEY GARDENS, HARROGATE.

The Kiosk Cafe and Tea and Coffee Stores,   The Cafe Imperial,

THE GROVE, ILKLEY. :::

Coffee a Speciality,
Roasted and Ground Daily.

For :::
High-Class Confectionery.

Only the Finest and
Purest Materials used.

PROPRIETORS: CHARLES TAYLOR & CO., 22, Park Row, LEEDS; ALSO 16, PARLIAMENT STREET, HARROGATE;
AND 52, WESTGATE, WAKEFIELD.

Taylors in the Valley Gardens
Municipal catering at its finest
at the beginning of the twentieth century

Fashionable Ilkley, 1900
The Kiosk Ilkley is now Bettys

Café Imperial :: Harrogate
Tel. No. 1243.

The Café Imperial, 1924

Taylors occupied the site of the present-day Bettys in Harrogate

Café Imperial
CE & CO LD

A gift from his staff

Charles Taylor's pocket watch

Taylors Tea

Taylors 'Pagoda Tea Tips' was the forerunner of 'Yorkshire Tea'

James Raleigh, 1907 — 1999

Taylors last chairman and tea taster extraordinaire

A Diamond Jubilee

17th July, 1979

Bettys celebrated its sixtieth anniversary in style. Having joined the family business four years earlier, I was put in charge of the celebrations.

There was music in the cafés, just as there had been in the days when Miss Maude Niner and Madame Cholmondeley-Harrop had held sway.

Customers who could find any pre-metric coinage could pay for their tea or coffee at 1919 prices.

We revived a whole collection of Frederick Belmont's fancies, which we hadn't made for years: 'Sarah Bernhardts', 'Chocolate Leopolds', and 'Mr Belmont's Kirsch Cigar' – best truffle, of course!

Betty's Ltd

The exclusive
CAFE
Under Royal and distinguished patronage.

SPECIAL NOTICE
We have engaged for the Winter Season
MISS MAUDE NINER,
Solo Violinists from the Queens Hall and Albert Hall,
London.
Accompaniste :
Mdme. **CHOLMONDELEY-HARROP.**

1921

There was a Diamond Jubilee Ball for 600 staff and their partners and a special Diamond Jubilee bonus equivalent to three months' pay for every member of staff.

I don't think we realized it at the time but Bettys Diamond Jubilee was the wake-up call for the third generation, and it shaped the way the business was to be run for the next twenty-five years. My wife Lesley joined the business then, followed by – for a few years at least – my brother Tony and my sister Elizabeth.

At the heart of our thinking was the desire to get right back in touch with the 'original sparks' that had ignited the ambitions of both Frederick Belmont and Charles Taylor. Both were craftsmen, driven perfectionists with an eye for detail. Yet both were visionaries, progressive – almost radical – in their thinking. Both would have been flattered to have their values treated with such respect by future generations; both would have been even more pleased to see their Swiss and Yorkshire heritage shaped and made contemporary by each generation.

Diamond Jubilee celebrations
Paraphernalia from July 1979

Bettys

DIAMOND JUBILEE BALL
at
Middlethorpe Hall York

THURSDAY 26 JULY 1979   8 PM - 1 AM

IN THE GARDEN

Barbeque & Buffet · Brass Band · Fairground Stalls · Steel Band

IN THE HALL

Dancing with two Discos and Steel Band · Three Bars · Pool Competition · Wine Bar

TICKETS

Staff -

Staff Tickets Free

Guests -
(only one per member of staff)
Husband/Wife Free
Other Guest £3·50

...ase sign ticket application list by   JULY 7

Kay and Victor Wild
At the Jubilee Ball

CHOCOLATE
LEOPOLD
rum & marzipan fancies

SARAH
BERNHARDT
*buttercream & fondant
fancies*

Curd Tarts
1½ᴰ each

Mr Belmont's fancies
Taken from his original recipe book

In the last twenty-five years, my generation has sought to resist the temptation to treat 'Bettys' and 'Taylors' as concepts or brands, but rather revere them as something more authentic. That's what we have tried to achieve, anyway; and I say 'we' because Bettys and Taylors in these decades has not just been about Lesley and me. My parents did not retire from the board until 1996, and, as well as my brother and sister, my cousin Valerie and her son Richard have all worked in the business and contributed enormously to its success.

It has not always been easy working together as a family. We are all rather sensitive, creative souls, but with that inherited single-minded competitive streak that sometimes leads to fall-outs. They say tension can be creative, but I prefer the harmony that prevails most of the time.

Nowadays the business is too diverse for one person, or even one family, to be experts at everything. Lesley and I have brought together and trained teams of some of the best craftsmen in the world: tea tasters, coffee masters, chocolatiers, bakers, confectioners, and cooks, and not forgetting the waiting staff who soothe your jangled nerves. Each generation of our craftsmen has to be more skilled than their predecessors: we couldn't survive otherwise.

We are still in the middle of the 'third generation years'. I am too close to it and so I don't want to write too much about it. It is still a colourful, living story and not ready to be captured as sepia-tinted history just yet.

Innovative as usual, 1927

COME TO A
YORKSHIRE
TEA TO-DAY

A NEW INNOVATION.

Betty's Ltd., beg to announce that they have introduced in their Cafe a little surprise for their many patrons in the form of a

YORKSHIRE TEA
AT AN INCLUSIVE COST OF **1/3**

Consisting of :—Tea or Coffee, with Cream; One Sandwich—Egg and Cress, York Ham or Potted Beef Steak; Special Yorkshire Teacake—toasted—or Hot Buttered Scone; One Cake—Plain, Fancy, or Cream.

This Tea is daintily served in the luxurious surroundings, which is exclusively " Betty's."

THE ORCHESTRA PLAYS FROM
3-30 to 5-30 DAILY.

Betty's Ltd

CAMBRIDGE
CRESCENT
HARROGATE,
AND AT
42 & 44, DARLEY STREET, BRADFORD.

THE
EXCLUSIVE
CAFE

Tea to suit the water: old-fashioned quality exported to twenty-nine countries

I will say that two things have characterized the years since Bettys Diamond Jubilee in 1979.

First has been learning to live with the success we have had taking Bettys expertise and products to a wider audience. We have never wanted to spoil the spirit of Bettys by turning her into a chain. Instead we have made specialist products like Yorkshire Tea, and sold them around the world. We never realised what an appetite there would be for old-fashioned quality.

Secondly, we have had to learn how to keep a family atmosphere in a business which now has over 1,000 staff. We have a wonderful leadership team, of which Lesley and I are only a small part. By staying solely Yorkshire based, we endeavour to preserve a family feel, but it is still our greatest challenge.

The Diamond Jubilee taught us to celebrate in style. Our annual staff ball is a grand affair, but a more practical celebration of success is the regular profit-sharing bonus paid to all our staff, even to newcomers and students. These are examples of the family's commitment to its extended family of staff: to their training, their welfare, their pride, and their pleasure.

Bettys generally appears calm, almost becalmed in its traditions. Not much for us to do, you might say, other than manage the queues. The reality is that we have to run very fast to appear to be standing still. One look at the changes to our menus over the years shows how hard we have to work to make our traditions contemporary in each generation. Tradition is a living thing, after all.

Bettys has always moved with the times, 1929

It is just over fifty years since my great-uncle Frederick Belmont died. I never knew him; I have no memories of him. He died when I was four months old.

I am sitting in his old office chair now. In front of me is his little smoking cabinet in which he kept his cigars. When I was born he gave my mother a gift to be kept and presented to me on my twenty-first birthday. It was a Jamaica Savana cigar. I smoked it at my birthday party.

The stewardship of his business was another gift, one which I have had to grow into over thirty years. It has been a real struggle for me and I forget how many times I have handed in my notice to my father!

If my great-uncle could come back down to earth just for one day, what would I want to show him of the present-day Bettys? Not just the buildings and traditions of his that we have preserved; those would flatter him but not stir him. No, what would excite – and I hope delight – him would be our newest ventures. But let's visit it all. Why not follow behind us...

CHAPTER 2

The Grand Tour

A visit to
Bettys Harrogate

From the swathes of crocuses which herald the spring, through to the autumn colours, the Stray is always a delight, and a window table at Bettys is the best place to enjoy it.

Harrogate is a treat to visit at any time of year. It is a floral town of great repute, with the 200-acre Stray parkland making what must be the biggest municipal front garden in Europe.

One of my abiding childhood memories is the excitement each October when the fairy lights in scores of Stray trees would be switched on. Fifty years later, the Stray illuminations are still a stylish spectacle every evening throughout the winter months.

It takes well over 100 staff to keep Bettys Harrogate open seven days and evenings a week. You'll see a lot of them sporting Bettys brooches: bronze for ten years' service, silver for twenty years, gold for thirty. It's a family affair, too, with several mothers and daughters and sons working together.

The young students you see working here aren't hired casuals. Typically they are with us for six years, helping to pay their way through school and university. They receive the same professional training as full-time staff. Some just can't bear to leave us; the rest set out into the big wide world with that bit of extra confidence, charm, capacity for hard work, and an eye for a good cake that only Bettys training brings!

You can't book a table at Bettys, so you will find celebrities queuing like everyone else. There are exceptions, such as when HRH The Prince of Wales asked if he could stop by for tea; his security put their foot down!

However busy we are, the queue still moves fast. As Uncle drummed into his staff from the early days: *'The most expensive thing in our business is an empty table.'*

A visit to
Bettys Cookery School

Lesley was outraged! As an A-stream student in the 1960s she had been denied cookery classes, but the thought that practical cookery skills had now been more or less sidelined from the whole of the national school curriculum was too much to bear.

Are there many other life skills as important as being able to cook for yourself, simply, safely, and cheaply? It was 2001 and time to make a dream come true. She would open a cookery school. Local schools could use it for free, the paying public would be taught by our own experts, and our staff could enjoy a training facility second to none.

Having been the director responsible for the tea room side of the business for many years, Lesley now focuses more of her attention around her cookery school and her lifelong love of cooking.

The school has been a great success. Although it looks dauntingly professional with eighteen workstations and a demonstration 'theatre', the atmosphere is so relaxed that the beginner and the experienced, the teenager and the granny work happily side by side.

Lesley's first attempt to teach cookery was thirty years ago in France when she showed her friend Beatrice how to make Yorkshire puddings. Using French ingredients, it was a disaster! Little did Lesley know that she had left one Yorkshire pudding in the back of the oven. Returning the following year we found a charred black object nailed to the kitchen wall. An inscription on the wall (politely translated here) ran: 'Fine example of typical English cooking.'

On that visit Beatrice served a less than perfect *tarte tartin*. Lesley resolved to become better than the French at this tricky dessert. Two decades later, she must make the best *tarte tartin* in the world. If you are lucky enough to be on a course when she is demonstrating it, you are in for a treat.

A visit to
Bettys at Harlow Carr Garden

Teaming up with the Royal Horticultural Society to open a Bettys at their beautiful gardens on the south-western outskirts of Harrogate is our latest enterprise.

Ever since Lesley opened her cookery school to provide opportunities for children to learn about real cooking, I have been searching for a partner for a similar project to enable children to learn about fruit and vegetables. That's how the conversation with the RHS started, and hopefully in time an educational kitchen garden will open. In the meantime we have created a stylish shop and café from which you can enjoy the lovely views whether or not you visit the garden itself.

Would Uncle approve of a Bettys in a garden? The Belmonts had a lovely garden but unlike my parents and I they were not 'hands-on' gardeners. They had a gardener called Spink. From his potting shed I salvaged a mirror advertising Jeyes Fluid, the disinfectant much beloved by old gardeners. Old Norman Brogden of Tockwith who taught me how to grow vegetables always

drenched young carrot plants with Jeyes Fluid to put the root-fly off the scent. I dutifully tried it. It prevented an infestation but the carrots reeked of Jeyes. That was what sent me organic!

Each Bettys has a different feel to it, reflecting the location and the building. At Harlow Carr, Lesley and her team have created a Bettys fit for an English country garden.

Harlow Carr was created in 1950 by northern gardeners as a place to trial plant varieties for their suitability in the challenging Yorkshire climate. Today it is a charming pleasure garden of over sixty-five acres for armchair gardeners as well as keen horticulturists. No matter if you get lost in its gardens: in a distant corner is another Bettys – a little wooden tea house offering simple refreshments through the warmer months.

A *visit to*
Bettys York

The city of York has so much history, and however long we are here, Bettys will always feel like a newcomer.

We occupy a privileged position right by the Lord Mayor's Mansion House. Across St Helen's Square, for the first forty years of its life, Bettys faced its great rival, Terry's Restaurant. Terry's had already been there for over 100 years before my great-uncle arrived in town, and many citizens thought Bettys an upstart. Only when Terry's closed in 1980 did Bettys become accepted as *the* place to meet in York. A weighty responsibility for us in such an important city.

With such wonderful monuments and museums, it takes a week to see everything. When you are ready for refreshment, head for Bettys; it is never far away.

The ground-floor tea room is a very public place, somewhere to watch the world go by through the elaborate stained-glass windows, or, as night falls, listen to the café pianist.

The basement Oakroom has stained glass too, but is most notable for its oak panelling which must have witnessed many a saucy wartime assignation in the days when it was Bettys Bar. In a corridor is the original 1940s' wartime mirror with its 500 etched signatures of servicemen, mostly Canadian aircrew.

Upstairs, the art deco Belmont function room is unchanged since the *Queen Mary* days.

Yes, memories abound in York. Alan is the longest-serving member of staff. I worked under him when he was head chef in the 1970s. Nowadays he works front of house as *maître d'*, and is the one to ask about the old days.

The ghost of Mrs Belmont is sighted from time to time. Why she prefers Bettys York I cannot explain, but she keeps everyone in good order!

A *visit to*
Little Bettys, York

Maybe because it's by far the oldest Bettys building, maybe because it is in historic Stonegate right opposite a snickleway called 'Coffee Yard', Little Bettys has the strongest feel of the old eighteenth-century coffee house about it.

Those London coffee houses were called 'penny universities' because they were great schools of conversation, wit, and learning, and the entrance fee was only a penny.

Long before it became Little Bettys, No. 46 Stonegate was called the Georgian Tearooms. Sixty years ago it was owned by Mr and Mrs Dick. Mr Dick was a shadowy figure who could be glimpsed standing by the big boiler in the kitchen. Mrs Dick busied herself serving tea and coffee at the ground and first-floor tables. Every now and then a young man, – sometimes two or three – would enter and disappear straight upstairs to the second floor. A bell would ring and Mrs Dick would climb the stairs with a trayful of coffee and toasted teacakes. This was York's 'penny university',

a private club for the intellectual élite of Nunthorpe Grammar School. They would discuss Shakespeare, the Classics in translation (even occasionally texts in Latin), and other less exalted topics, and every now and then pull a rope to ring the bell to summon Mrs Dick with fresh refreshments. John Langton, the well-known York artist, was a member of this club in the late 1940s and told me the story.

In the 1960s the new university in York provided a fresh intellectual clientele; obviously very fresh indeed, because since that era the cosy room at the back of the café has been known as 'Lovers' Corner'!

Little Bettys still has university links and it's not unusual to see a professor or two taking tea.

**CAFÉ
TEA ROOM
UPSTAIRS**

Little Bettys

A visit to
Bettys Ilkley

Ilkley is many people's favourite Bettys. Blessed with a lovely Wharfedale location, the shop looks south towards Ilkley Moor and the café north towards Middleton Moor. In between the two views is a team of eighty of the most friendly, professional Bettys staff you are likely to meet.

If one or two of the youngsters are concentrating so hard they can barely smile, please forgive them. Learning the 'Bettys way' of doing things requires exacting training... and practice, practice, practice. Even the simplest task, such as laying up a tea tray, has five pages of precise detail in the training book. With experience these details become second nature, and the smile gets bigger and bigger.

Like Harrogate, Ilkley is a spa town with a real country feel. Its myriad of small independent shops are a good reason to visit the town for the day. More than anything else though, Ilkley is a place to walk!

The riverside and the lower reaches of Ilkley Moor were tamed with good paths in Victorian times. Beyond are the crags and the famous Cow and Calf rocks. A group of us from Bettys once set out to prove our Yorkshire grit by abseiling down the overhanging cliff of the Cow. Never again!

More my cup of tea are the wild moors that stretch beyond, both to the north and to the south of the town. You can even walk all the way to Harrogate, fifteen miles away, on high ground. Breakfast at one Bettys, high tea at the other, with a great day's walking in between. I know it can be done; I've done it myself! But please don't forget to leave your muddy boots at the door!

A *visit to*
Bettys Northallerton

My father moved Bettys from Leeds here to the county town of North Yorkshire in 1971 when life in the city became too fraught and expensive.

His new premises were cosy but cramped, with not enough room for the queues. Thirty-three years later Lesley spotted the potential of a semi-derelict listed Georgian building nearby, and, after a year of restoration, the new Bettys has 'just opened'.

On opening day we were all as excited as Uncle was back in July 1919 when the first Bettys opened in Harrogate.

Bettys Northallerton is as beautiful, as elegant, and as cosy as Uncle would have wished, with a Palm Room and an outdoor garden courtyard as well as the traditional tea room. In the shop is a coffee bar where coffee, cakes, and sandwiches are served to those in more of a hurry.

Northallerton certainly is a bustling town, with a thriving market taking over the high street in front of Bettys on Wednesdays and Saturdays and with other family businesses to provide a welcome respite from chain outlets.

Of course Northallerton is worth visiting in its own right, but it is also on the way to... well, everywhere! A perfect end to a day in Wensleydale or Swaledale to the west, or a start to a day on the North York Moors or Whitby on the coast to the east. Being only a few miles from the A1, Bettys Northallerton is a welcoming antidote to a motorway service station on any long journey to the north or south.

One trip to Northallerton and I think Uncle would forgive and even congratulate us for closing his Leeds café and moving here, just as he would applaud us for moving out of Bradford to the country air of Ilkley.

10am – First stop Bettys in York for breakfast!

11am – Next on to Little Bettys, and just in time for elevenses!

Vic and Linda make a stop to enjoy the view over the Dales

A Grand Day Out

This chapter is dedicated to our regular customers, Victor and Linda Burton. To celebrate their twenty-fifth wedding anniversary they decided to visit every Bettys branch in one day, travelling on a Harley Davidson motorbike. It sounds like the perfect cure for anyone's midlife crisis!

They have inspired me to start to put together a book of journeys around and between Bettys Tea Rooms, by car, bike, and on foot.

In the boot of my car, for the last twenty years, I have carried a rucksack full of walking clothes. I have this dream that one sunny day on my way to work at Ilkley or Northallerton, I will run away to the hills for the day. Alas, duty is a powerful presence in a family business, and I have never used my 'running-away rucksack'... yet! Now I have an excuse... research!

If you have any favourite routes to suggest, including the best way of visiting all six Bettys branches in one day, then please write to me. I will research them personally and at last my 'running-away rucksack' will be put to good use.

It always surprises me how many people regularly visit three or four different Bettys branches. It surprises me even more how many people just stick to their one favourite Bettys.

The map here is a reminder of how wonderfully situated all the Bettys Tea Rooms are. Never far from the Yorkshire Dales and the North York Moors National Parks, Bettys have the best landscapes in the country on their doorstep. Yet the conurbations of Leeds, Bradford, even Manchester and east Lancashire, are not too far away. No wonder my great-uncle decided to 'stay a while'.

We constantly receive letters suggesting we open a Bettys in such-and-such a town or city, in the UK and overseas. My reply is always that for such a self-sufficient business as ours it is not practical for daily deliveries to be more than thirty miles from our bakery.

There is another reason, too. One of the few pieces of my father's advice I have listened to is: *'Don't open a business anywhere you are not prepared to travel once a week, and enjoy the journey.'*

The special intimacy of Bettys requires us all to be in close contact: to spread ourselves widely would risk spoiling that – except of course, that little hotel in the Swiss Alps I keep dreaming of! Now that would be a grand day out on a Harley motorbike!

1.00pm – Next to Bettys in
Northallerton for lunch

3.00pm – A whistle-stop in Harrogate…
for tea and a tart!

5pm – Arrive in style at Bettys Ilkley
for high tea

CHAPTER 3

Behind the Scenes

◆

Behind the scenes at the Tea Rooms

There is more going on behind the scenes at a Bettys tea room than you can imagine. With as many as 140 staff per tea room, back-of-house is like a small village. However, it is not like the 'below stairs' of the old days.

Service is not servitude and staff expect to have as pleasant facilities as their customers. Free food and drinks, newspapers, radio, TV, and internet help them relax and recharge their batteries. Serving your needs is mentally and physically demanding, but you rarely hear anyone letting off steam behind the scenes. It really is a friendly place; everyone says it's the best bit about working at Bettys.

Peep through the kitchen doors, and you will see gleaming modern kitchens; our practices are rather old-fashioned though. Lesley won't allow microwave ovens in our kitchens; if things need cooking, they get cooked the time-honoured way, in pans or under grills. Proper

food deserves proper respect, Lesley argues. We see ourselves as cooks, not chefs, and it is in the art of wholesome cooking that we train our staff.

However much we all clean as we go, we still need a team of housekeepers to tidy up after us. As if they weren't busy enough already, what with aprons to iron, silverware and brassware to polish, and cloakrooms to service.

Can you imagine how many items our dishwashing team wash on a busy Saturday? Over 7,000 at Bettys Harrogate alone! It's the one department where service does sometimes feel like servitude! I know from my own experience.

Behind the scenes at
Bettys Craft Bakery

Half close your eyes for just a moment, and you could be in Switzerland not Harrogate. A Swiss chalet of a bakery, troughs of geraniums… and an ancient cowbell in the foyer to ring for attention.

The Bread and Pastry Rooms

Bakers working off bread doughs on wooden tables, and shaping pastries on a great marble slab. A wood-fired oven, not a flimsy metal slab-framed one that you might see in a pizzeria but a mighty one, insulated with ten tons of river sand maintaining a soothing evenness of heat that bakes a loaf to crusty perfection.

Perfection? Not quite. Every day, every loaf is ever so slightly different: a sign that humans and not machines are in control. Of course

Bettys bakers have the best of technology: mixers, computer-monitored provers, and so on; but as with 100 years ago, it is the baker and not his tools that makes or breaks the bread.

Johann Bützer, my great-grandfather, might recognize the hefty Swiss Breakfast Loaves and Fitness Bread but he would be bemused by the Yorkshire Cobbles, Mouse Bread, and Fat Rascals, a fusion of two baking traditions that seems perfectly natural to my generation.

The Chocolate and Confectionery Rooms

In this part of the bakery, away from the ovens and the smell of baking, the eyes take over from the nose. Even the heady aroma of melted chocolate is barely noticed as visitors look in awe at craftsmanship which, around most of the world, died out decades ago.

At 6am the confectioners are finishing all the fresh cream cakes and fresh fruit flans, a race against time to be ready for the van departure deadline of 7.30am. Then it's on to all the different fancies, which have to be produced in stages over two or three days. Often they start out as huge slabs, only taking shape in the final stages.

According to the seasons the confectioners can find themselves making deliciously sweet apples, carrots, pumpkins and pigs, Santas and snowmen. Meanwhile the cake-decorating team make every conceivable kind of flower by hand to adorn wedding cakes and Easter eggs: sweet peas, pansies, violets and lilies, brambles, roses, and daffodils. It's the edible country garden of every child's dreams.

Come rain or shine, the Chocolate Room is held at a constant temperature of 18°C. Chocolate is like a naughty child: having coaxed and cajoled it into good 'temper', all smooth and glossy with a crisp snap, you only have to turn your back for a moment for it to lose its temper and go grainy, blotchy, and 'bloomy'. Susceptible to heat and cold, draughts and damp, the only way to get chocolate to behave is to give it no excuse to misbehave! A constant 18°C does the trick.

The artistry does not end here: the chocolate-packing team are craftsmen too, tying ribbons and bows with mesmerizing dexterity, and wearing white cotton gloves to polish Bettys golden guineas to perfection.

Then there are the fillings: praline, caramel, fresh cream, and champagne, delicate flavours which do not overpower the palate, all piped carefully by hand. Bettys chocolates must be good for you: just look at how healthy and slim the chocolatiers are!

In the 1920s, Uncle used to advertise Bettys chocolates as a slimming aid and a cure for weak hearts!

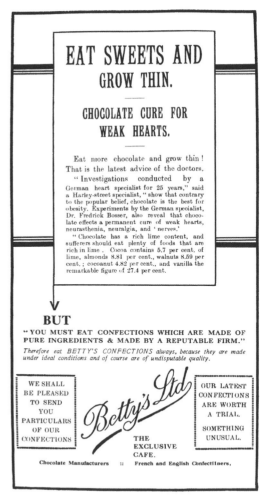

1929

Behind the scenes at
Bettys by Post

I would love to be able to take Uncle to visit our mail-order department, Bettys by Post. I know he would be thrilled to see his dream come true – at last.

Uncle had always offered a mailing service at Bettys shops, but in 1935 he decided to set up a serious mail-order chocolate business. *'We have sent out 5,000 circulars',* he wrote in his diary. The result of the mail shot was *'disappointing; about thirty orders'.* The first envelope he opened contained a postal order for 18/3d. The second contained a request for 3d. *'No stamp on the envelope... rather humorous... I wonder what will become of this department?'* See for yourself, Uncle! You were simply ahead of your time!

Seventy years later it's a thriving department with twenty staff, despatching orders all over the world. Over a third of the orders are nowadays received over the internet. We still prefer the personal contact when our customers phone us up!

Bettys by Post despatches over 25,000 parcels a year, from £100 hampers to small but regular supplies of tea and coffee to homesick Yorkshire souls in foreign parts, from Southend to Sydney.

Christmas is our busiest time with at least 100 products to choose from in our festive catalogue. But birthdays occur 365 days a year and celebration cakes, chocolate tortes, and children's party cakes are despatched every day. When you get a parcel from Bettys by Post, you know someone thinks you are very special!

1928

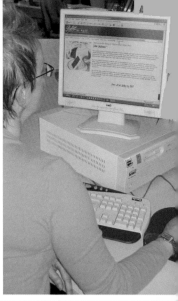

Behind the scenes at
Taylors of Harrogate

Is there the faintest of aromas of apples and pears in your tea? For me there always will be, because when my father decided to move the newly acquired Taylors tea and coffee warehouse and roastery to Harrogate, he felled Bettys Bakery's orchard to make room for it.

I sense the orchard as a presence still haunting Plumpton Park, the site Bettys Bakery, Taylors of Harrogate, and now Bettys Cookery School too, share to this day.

In the old warehouse in Leeds, back in Charles Taylor's day, they would handle 4,000 sacks, chests, and barrels of tea and coffee a year. Today we import nearly 200,000 a year. It takes a team of 250 staff to buy, blend, roast, pack, and distribute it.

The list of tropical countries and islands we import from whets the appetite for an exotic holiday: India, Sri Lanka, China, Japan, Kenya, Ethiopia, Rwanda, Burundi, Tanzania, South Africa, Brazil, Colombia, Peru, Costa Rica, Nicaragua, Guatemala, Mexico, Cuba, Jamaica, Java, and Sumatra, each producing their own unique-tasting beverage according to the soil, the climate, the harvesting method, and the strain of plant.

It seems like very hard work, but all these countries have to be visited... regularly! It takes a team of seven buyers to share the burden, but this direct personal contact with the growers of our tea and coffee is crucial. Without it there is no mutual trust and understanding, no opportunity to secure the pick of the crop, no way of establishing realistic, ethical, fair trading relationships.

We don't just pay top prices to be charitable: it is all about rewarding quality and recognizing growers who are dedicated to putting in the extra effort and attention to detail. In these circumstances it's a pleasure to pay the best prices and present much-appreciated enamel 'Rewarding Quality' plaques.

In recent years the world has been flooded with cheap coffee and this has led to severe hardship for most of the world's coffee farmers. In many cases the selling price has been well below the cost of production. Little wonder coffee plantations were abandoned or uprooted. If the farmers are committed to top quality, we can help them. Our Sustainable Buying Programme ensures farmers cover their costs and make some profit. In exchange, the farmers undergo social audits to ensure that all workers are treated properly. Four of our buyers are qualified to audit to the standards of the Ethical Trading Initiative.

When they are not travelling our buyers have even more serious work to do. The two tasting rooms – one for tea, one for coffee – are the homes of extraordinary skill, creativity, and craftsmanship.

There is the discipline and concentrated effort of tasting up to 300 teas a day, judging quality, detecting faults, looking for nuances of character, body, colour, and flavour, and assessing their potential to brew better in either hard or soft water.

There is the skill of putting together blends, for the perfect cup of tea or coffee is often a complex blend of different origins, each one selected to bring a particular characteristic to the whole. As the seasons change in different parts of the world, so must the components of our blends change, and yet you, our customer, must get your favoured flavour consistently throughout the year.

Then there is the creativity of inventing new blends. Although we are a very traditional business, we thrive on the stimulus of new ideas. I think that creating blends successfully depends on wisdom rather than cleverness. There is no substitute for years (and years) of training to develop the deep knowledge and understanding of these extraordinary tropical commodities.

Back in 1962 when he took over the tiny Taylors tea and coffee business, my father had no idea that forty years later our buying skills would be in such demand. It was never really our intention, but the public's appreciation for what we do has taken our Taylors products far beyond Bettys.

Our Yorkshire Tea is the nation's best-selling top-quality tea, and similarly our roast and ground coffees set the quality standard for the coffee market. We export to twenty-nine countries including the USA, Australia, Canada, Japan, and across Europe.

I have to confess that Yorkshire Tea nearly wasn't called Yorkshire. When the printer's proofs of the first packaging were shown to the directors, they all nodded their approval and it was duly minuted. It was only after the meeting that an error was spotted by our tea-buying director, Warren Ford, the best tea man of his generation. On all six faces of the box, 'Yorkshire' was spelt without the 'k'. I doubt 'Yorshire Tea' would have proved so popular. In fact, it would have been a monumental disaster.

However successful we are, we will never be the biggest, but our buying team will always strive to be the best. We always keep some of our rarest finds exclusively to Bettys and Bettys by Post. You can always be assured of ordering a pot of something in our café which literally no one else in the world will be drinking. That's a nice feeling.

Meanwhile, if you fancy a career with our buying team it does help to be able to ride a horse, as buyer Kate found recently in Peru, when horseback was the only way to get to a remote coffee farm which had never had a visitor before.

Our tea and coffee factory is like no factory you would imagine. Ours is no gloomy place. There are huge windows everywhere to let the sunshine in, and, right in the middle, a lush Tropical House, bursting with flowering tea, coffee, and cocoa plants which my father has raised from seed.

Blending a dozen different teas together, a ton at a time, is a gentle process. A large drum tumbles the teas in just eight slow rotations, so the leaf is not damaged. Teas with flowers and scents are blended in much smaller batches, and very special teas are inspected almost leaf by leaf by Andrew before they end up on the tea counter at Bettys.

Nowadays, most people want their tea in convenient tea-bag form. In the Yorkshire Tea Hall, very clever machines (run by even cleverer engineers) pack the tea into bags, and thence into boxes, faster than you can blink.

Coffee has to be roasted as well as blended. We still use basically the same technology of a rotating drum with a gas flame that we used fifty, even 100 years ago. Of course, there is still a good, slow, even roast, with infinite possibilities to roast darker or lighter to suit the particular blend.

Although grinding coffee beans in your own kitchen creates an aroma almost as delectable as drinking the coffee itself, most people want the convenience of ready-ground coffee. Preserving the aroma is the most important thing and we have the best technology to do just that.

In our shops we grind beans straight into the bag; in the coffee hall we do just the same, but here flushing away all the air as we seal the coffee into airtight bags. Being so fresh, the coffee continues to give off roasting gases for some time and would explode the bag if it wasn't for the cunning little one-way valve on the front of the pack. It's the oxygen in the air that stales coffee and ruins the aroma, so always keep your coffee airtight and cool!

All this technology is a far cry from the early days. In my teenage years I could never understand how so many bits of my Meccano set went missing. When I joined the business and started training at Taylors I discovered that half the machines were held together with my Meccano! My father was his own chief engineer in those days.

Back in 1976, I remember spending weeks and weeks packing our first export order. It was for Egypt. Tens of thousands of packets of tea were labelled 'Camel Brand' in Arabic, and were then packed into chests tied with special straps so the merchants could attach them to camels and take them out into the desert to sell the tea to the nomads.

Life at Taylors is still an extraordinary whirl of importing and exporting. One or two things are home grown, though. The crop from our own Tropical House is very small, but a cup of Harrogate-grown coffee or tea is something really special. For those in the know, the Tropical House is a fitting monument to the memory of Uncle's orchard.

You pass by our Plumpton Park site on the train from Harrogate to York, just between Starbeck and the aptly named Belmont Crossing. Look out for a giant teapot clock. If your train is running exactly to time the clock is programmed to pour before your very eyes!

'Camel' teapot

Trees for Life

It all started with *Blue Peter*, the BBC children's programme which has done so much to prompt social and environmental awareness amongst the young. My own children were avid viewers, and in the period after the 1984 Ethiopian drought, and with it a growing awareness of the impact of global deforestation and the destruction of the rainforest, they asked me what we as a family could do. 'If you plant the first tree,' I told them, 'I will find a way of planting nine hundred and ninety-nine thousand, nine hundred and ninety-nine more.'

So began our 'Trees for Life' environmental campaign. We enlisted help from our loyal Yorkshire Tea drinkers, from schools, from Women's Institutes, and slowly but surely the funds came in. I dreamt we could get to a million trees in one year; in fact it took ten.

In the early years we concentrated on Ethiopia, scene of those terrible famines in the 1980s. Through our charity partners, particularly Oxfam, we learned that new forests couldn't survive without stable communities willing and able to look after them. We broadened our support to include general social and environmental projects, but always with a tree element involved.

We have kept faith with Ethiopia but also extended our reach to tree projects all around the world, particularly in those countries which grow our tea and coffee.

Women's Institutes are still great supporters of our work, and in one year alone they collected enough tokens to have a 200-acre, 30,000-tree plantation named after them in Ethiopia.

Closer to home we have supported many tree-planting projects in Yorkshire. We even plant a tree for every child or grandchild born to a member of staff, and celebrate with 'Babes in the Wood' picnics.

Even allowing for a huge number of failures, our tree-planting total reached two million in 2003. HRH The Prince of Wales planted an oak tree commemorating the achievement in front of Bettys Harrogate.

If you hunt around, you will find three more commemorative 'Trees for Life' trees near Bettys, each marking a stage in our tree-planting journey.

Two million trees is not enough to save the planet, but it goes some way to compensate for the carbon emissions Bettys and Taylors make, and, as a wise man once said: 'The greatest mistake is made by he who, because he can do only a little, does nothing.'

We commit on average five per cent of our annual profits to environmental and community projects, both global and local. It's one of the reasons why staff are so proud to work for Bettys and Taylors.

But the money has come from you, our customers, in the first place, and you have every reason to take some pride yourself. £1 from the sale of this book will go to our 'Trees for Life' fund. Somewhere around the world you have just helped plant a tree.

'Trees for Life' tree biscuits

YORKSHIRE TEA 'TREES FOR LIFE'

1st of a MILLION

Planted by HRH The Prince of Wales
on 14th February 2003
to commemorate the two million
trees planted around the world by
Bettys & Taylors of Harrogate
"Trees for Life"
1990 - 2001

YORKSHIRE TEA
'TREES FOR LIFE'

LAST of a MILLION

CHAPTER 4

The Treasures of Bettys

THE TREASURES OF BETTYS
Marquetry

Uncle spent far too much money on his premises in his efforts to create what in his adverts he called: *'surroundings with the quiet harmony of perfect taste'*. On display at Bettys Harrogate and Ilkley is his collection of exquisite marquetry pictures from the studio of Charles Spindler in Alsace, France.

Charles Spindler founded his studio in the late 1890s at the height of the art nouveau period. Instead of using marquetry just to make pretty floral pictures on furniture, he used natural unstained veneers, collected from around the world, to create literally 'paintings in wood'.

His son, Paul, an equally talented artist and craftsman, joined him in the studio in the early 1920s. Paul's son, Jean-Charles, followed suit in the 1970s and still runs the studio in the tiny village of St Leonard, surrounded by vineyards against the backdrop of the forested Vosges mountains.

When Uncle discovered Spindler's work in the early 1930s he bought a few pieces for his own 'den' at home. In 1934 he commissioned the studio to make six large pictures of Yorkshire scenes to hang in Bettys Harrogate. Young Paul Spindler travelled over and drew the sketches from which the evocative pieces that hang in the Harrogate 'Spindler Room' were made.

Lesley and I made contact with the family again in 1976 and over the years added to his collection, including the largest marquetry picture ever made in the studio, 'La Chasse' ('The Hunt') – which hangs in Bettys Ilkley.

Fountains Abbey

Ripon

Burnt Yates

Bolton Abbey

Knaresborough

La Chasse

Jean-Charles serves us tea at his home in St Leonard

Spindler

Bootham Bar, York – one of the six Yorkshire scenes, commissioned in 1934

Paul Spindler sketching in York

Creating a marquetry, a jigsaw constructed of tiny pieces precisely cut from different woods

The initial sketch of York

AMBOINA

ASH

BURANO

BUBINGA

DALOA

PEROBA

MAHOGANY

NEGLINDO

OAK

KNOBBY OAK

PLANE

POPLAR

TAMARIND

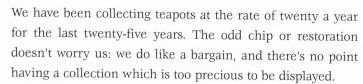

We have been collecting teapots at the rate of twenty a year for the last twenty-five years. The odd chip or restoration doesn't worry us: we do like a bargain, and there's no point having a collection which is too precious to be displayed.

My mother, Kay, has found many of the teapots in the collection, which ranges from 1750 to the present day.

We particularly seek out strange inventions, like the Earl of Dundonald's 'Simple Yet Perfect' pot, patented in 1901, which enables you to tilt the pot on its side after five minutes to separate the tea infusion chamber from the brew.

'Patent Self-Pourer'

'Simple Yet Perfect'

Then there is J. J. Royle's 'Patent Self-Pourer' of 1886, which enables the genteel hostess to pour the tea without lifting the teapot, by means of a cunning pump concealed in the lid.

We have several 'Cadogan' teapots, attributed to Lady Cadogan who in the 1830s liked to amuse her guests with a teapot with no visible means of getting the tea into the pot: it was filled through the base!

'Cadogan'

'Empire Clock'

For music lovers there is the 'Musical' teapot, which plays whenever the pot is lifted, while for travellers there is the 'Empire Clock' teapot: by swivelling the lid you can tell what time it is in any part of the British Empire.

The Cunard steamship company devised the 'Cube', a teapot whose rebated handle and spout would survive any storm.

For Women's Institutes there is a pot with two spouts to deal with a thirsty queue all the quicker.

'Musical'

'Cunard Cube'

There is one we don't have – and which I have never seen – which was patented in 1812 by one Sarah Guppy, the wife of a Bristol merchant. An egg is suspended in a casket inside the pot so that by the time your tea is brewed, your breakfast egg is boiled! If you've got one let me know – please!

Animals abound in our collection – my favourites are the 'Minton Monkey' and the 'Panda' – as do commemoratives from the Battle of Trafalgar to the present.

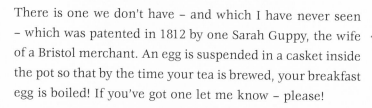

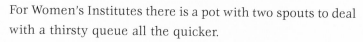

'Women's Institute'

'Battle of Trafalgar'

'Emily Pankhurst'

Our collection of caricatures and satirical teapots includes 'Emily Pankhurst', who reminds me of my great aunt Liseli, who was a Swiss suffragette. The first teapot I ever bought was a Greatbach 'Prodigal Son'. Once addicted, the teapot I really, really wanted was a very rare caricature of Oscar Wilde, one of the nicknames I had to endure at school! It is called the 'Aesthetic'. My mother heard that one of these was up for auction by Sotheby's in Sussex. We had never paid anything remotely like £1,000 for a teapot before, but that is what I gave her to secure this gem. On the train down to Sussex she was joined in the compartment by a man who coincidentally was going to the same auction. He had never been to an auction before, but a friend of his, anxious to impress a girlfriend, wanted to obtain a particular piece of china for her and he had been given £6,000 in cash. My mother patiently explained to the novice how auctions worked and how to bid.

On arriving at the small country station, my mother found the taxi she had pre-booked. The man had made no such arrangements and there was no way he was going to get to the auction on time. Kay took pity on him and gave him a lift. In the taxi she asked him the question she knew she had to ask. 'Which piece of china are you bidding for?' She knew the answer before he replied. 'It's something called the "Aesthetic" – it's to do with Oscar Wilde.' Guess who got the teapot?

There is a happy ending. Hearing my mother's sad tale, a collector parted with his slightly chipped 'Aesthetic' at a knock-down price!

'Prodigal Son'

'Panda'

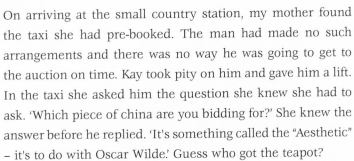

'Minton Monkey'

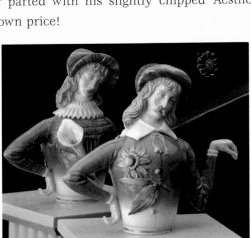

The two-faced slightly chipped 'Aesthetic'
with the reverse side cleverly reflected in a mirror

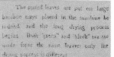

These girls are sorting the small tender leaves from the larger and coarser ones. It is tiresome work but the social occasion afforded is no little compensation

The sorted leaves are put on large bamboo trays placed in the sunshine to be dried and the long drying process begins. Both "green" and "black" tea are made from the same leaves only the drying process is different

Little Bettys is the place to see examples from our large collection of prints, advertisements, and paraphernalia which tell the story of the tea trade.

Currently on display is a series of Japanese and Chinese prints. The most extraordinary one shows monkeys being used to pluck leaves from wild tea bushes on inaccessible crags. Another shows women using chopsticks to sort out the best leaves.

SEPARATING THE LEAVES
AFTER FIRING

"Wake up and have a cup of Tea"

HARVEY BROS. & TYLER, LONDON.

COMPLIMENTS
OF THE
ORIENTAL
COFFEE HOUSE CO.

Carved ebony box presented to Edward, Prince of Wales, on his visit to Ceylon in 1875

'Sold to the man with more money than sense!'

The treasure that means the most to me is not on display. It brings back shameful memories.

It is the very last chest of tea sold in the London tea auction following its closure after 319 years of weekly auctions. London was for so long the most important auction in the world, but as the shift in tea consumption has moved to the Middle East, it is the auctions in the growing regions – Mombasa, Calcutta, Colombo, and Jakarta – that have taken over.

Our tea-buying team graciously awarded me the privilege of representing the company on this historic occasion on 29th June, 1998. Little did they realize that I would pay the highest price ever recorded for a single chest of tea: £18,315!

Fifteen companies started the bidding for the very last lot: one chest of Hellbodde Estate Ceylon Flowery Pekoe. By the time the price had escalated to £5,000, it was down to John Leeder of Twinings and myself. What with all the TV cameras and photographers there, I'm afraid 'auction fever' possessed me. Anyway, I was absolutely convinced that the rightful home for this treasure was in Yorkshire. It was all for charity, so how could I be blamed if I kept on bidding and bidding?

As penance, I have not bid in any kind of auction since! Correction: I have not been *allowed* to bid in any kind of auction since!

We were one of the first companies to win a Queen's Award for Enterprise for Sustainable Development. We were very proud to have all our community work and tree-planting around the world recognized as something special. Sally Holme, our managing director, went to Buckingham Palace together with two staff, Andrew and Marion. They stood in line and were presented to the Queen and Prince Philip. Straight afterwards, an equerry approached Sally and said that the Queen would like to have further private words with the Bettys party.

'Oh no,' thought Sally, 'She is going to ask whether Bettys is named after her mother!' Sally rushed to the powder room to practise her reply in front of a mirror. True, some people have speculated that Bettys was named after the young Elizabeth Bowes-Lyon, but it is unlikely. Should she please Her Majesty by confirming the story as true, or tell her the truth? Sally rehearsed her diplomatic answer: 'Your Majesty, the young Frederick Belmont was quite a ladies' man. Was by any chance your mother, in her younger days, one for the gentlemen?' In the event Her Majesty asked every kind of question – except the one that Sally had rehearsed the answer to!

'It's alright, we've brought our own tea!'
Marion, Andrew, and Sally

The oldest medal in our collection is a gold medal for coffee roasting won by Charles Taylor at the London Grocery Exhibition of 1896. The earliest surviving medal won by Frederick Belmont was from the International Confectionery Exhibition of 1928, but we treasure more his 'passing-out' certificate of 1903 from the Swiss Master Bakers' Association.

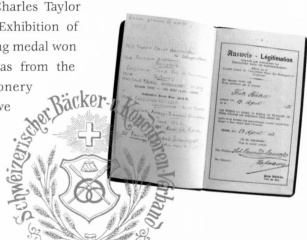

Our bakery team have won many medals since, but 2004 brought a particularly fine harvest with national awards for youngsters Joanne Sanderson (for bread and pastry) and Helen Barker (for patisserie) and the national 'Craft Bakery of the Year' for the whole bakery team. Not to be outdone, our café teams have won twenty-six Awards of Excellence

from the Tea Council and 'Top Tea Place of the Year' on three occasions.

I've never been to an Oscars-style award ceremony myself and so don't really understand the pressure on the nominees on the night.

Katy Squire, our Trees for Life champion, represented us at a Business in the Community awards dinner. She was so sure we wouldn't win that she didn't even buy a new frock. Much to her horror her name was called and a spotlight followed her to the stage. She was so disorientated that she couldn't find the steps. She hoisted herself up on to the stage with her hands and knees, and in front of an audience of thousands did her best to look cool and poised as she collected the award

and an oak sapling. I was on a moonlight stroll through an Italian olive grove with Lesley when the call from Katy came through. 'Did you win?' I gasped. Still totally confused, all she could say was: 'I'm not sure, I think so!'

Some awards need us all to pull together year after year to win. It has required a huge commitment to teamwork and personal development by all the Bettys and Taylors staff to win National Training Awards, Investors in People, the British Safety Council Sword of Honour, and Best Companies to Work For.

Katy's oak sapling

It has been a great boost to confidence to receive these awards over the years – and we treasure them dearly – but what makes us all most proud is the recognition we receive every day from loyal customers who choose to spend their money with us. Now that's what we call praise!

An arduous wine tasting in the vineyard

Our most precious treasure of all is our heritage. Although we are now really a Yorkshire family, our Swiss heritage still has an enormous impact on the way the business is run. Whether it is Swiss products, Swiss techniques, or simply Swiss precision, finesse, and attention to detail, Switzerland still has a clear voice in our culture.

To keep that voice alive and resonant, each year Lesley takes a group of staff to eat and drink their way round Switzerland. In the cities the group visit smart cafés, bakeries, and chocolate shops and go out to dinner with my Swiss cousin Nelli. In the mountains they make a pilgrimage to the wonderful Ruedihus in Kandersteg to taste traditional rustic dishes, or journey to Pontresina in the Engadine where my father trained after the war, and where the Kochendörfer and Walther families always make us welcome.

The Ruedihus

Sprüngli, Zürich

Visiting the mill at Wangen-an-der-Aare where our family story begins is always emotional, but a tasting at the Bonvin family vineyard, from where we import all our Swiss wine, soon cheers everyone up.

The mill at Wangen-an-der-Aare

Nearly 2,000 feet up, on a craggy outcrop overlooking the Rhone valley, surrounded by snow-capped mountains, this really is a vineyard with a difference. Mountain weather can be treacherous, but here in southern Switzerland the weather is perfect for vines, with long hot summers merging into autumn. It never gets too hot because at about two o'clock in the afternoon a cooling breeze starts to waft down the valley from the Rhone glacier at its head. The Bonvin wines we import are really too good, too special to be 'house wines', but we can't resist.

A vineyard with a difference

Switzerland draws heavily from the culture of its neighbours, Italy, France, Germany, and Austria, and we too stray over the borders in our influences.

Just to the north, in France, is the region of Alsace, home to the Spindler marquetry family. Jean-Charles Spindler married into the Muller family and for more than twenty years now we have imported their wonderful wines. Madeline Muller heads the firm of Jean-Jacques Muller, helped by daughter Beatrice. Alsace makes the best white wines in the world, better even than the Swiss.

Beatrice Muller amongst her family's 'grand cru' vines in Alsace

A Zürich shop window

Italy has always been a strong influence on us, and Lesley takes her groups south to Milan to visit Peck's food hall and the famous café Cova – which serves our tea! Whether it's Venetian festival cake, Siennese panforte, pannetone, or rustic breads, we always go back to authentic recipes and then give them a Bettys twist, which we hope you'll agree makes them better than the mass-produced ones which are imported into this country.

Bettys shop window

That's enough travelling for now! I must admit that one of our dreams is to open a Bettys hotel in the Swiss mountains, so we can all take turns to work there for a month or two each year! Hmmm... maybe we should just stick to what we know we are good at.

Spot the site for Bettys...

CHAPTER 5

Who Was Betty?

Who Was Betty?

1st August: today is Yorkshire Day, when we wear our white roses with extra pride. Seven hundred miles away on the same day the Swiss are celebrating Swiss National Day. On this day of double celebration for a Swiss-Yorkshire business, it seems a good time to enquire whether 'Betty' was Swiss or Yorkshire.

Whilst all our family plead ignorance, everyone else has their own theory about the elusive Betty. I receive letters on the subject quite regularly, always quite plausible accounts of how somebody's great-grandmother Elizabeth – or Lilibet if Swiss – was an intimate friend of Frederick Belmont a century ago.

One sentimental story claims that Frederick called Bettys after the daughter of the doctor who practised next door to the new café premises. The young girl was dying of TB and Frederick said he would immortalize her name forever.

Betty Lupton, 'Queen of the Wells'

The next story is almost too obvious to be true. The most famous character in the history of Harrogate was Betty Lupton. For nearly sixty years from 1778 Betty was in charge of dispensing the sulphur waters to visitors to the spa. She and her assistants were called 'ladlers' or 'nymphs'. Betty was known as 'Chief Nymph' until, in June 1838, on the very day of Queen Victoria's coronation, Betty herself was crowned 'Queen of the Harrogate Wells'. Did Frederick decide to endear himself to the Harrogate population by calling his café after their spa 'Queen'? We have in our collection Betty Lupton's own cup and saucer, passed on by one of her descendents who was convinced of the veracity of this tale.

Here are two much more likely stories. I have researched them thoroughly. They could be true; I would quite like them to be true. You decide.

A few years ago a lady telephoned to say that she had some gossip about Betty that she had been dying to tell me for years; only her mother had always forbidden her to divulge such tittle-tattle.

Back in the 1950s her family had moved to Harrogate and lived in lodgings owned by a Miss Firth. Miss Firth had revealed the secret to her mother.

Miss Firth, my Auntie Hilda! Not a real aunt but my great-aunt Bunny Belmont's best friend. My abiding memory of her is after Christmas dinner every year, when she would settle, just a little tipsy, in an armchair and start to recite from memory the *Rubaiyat of Omar Khayyam*, the epic poem. Our challenge was to distract her as quickly as possible before she got into her stride and get her to play 'passing the matchbox from nose to nose' or 'relay racing with a balloon between the knees'.

Betty Howe

Auntie Hilda almost appeared in an earlier chapter – 2nd October, 1952. Auntie Bunny was round at Auntie Hilda's having her usual Saturday pre-lunch martini at the very moment when Dickie Belmont had his heart attack. At that same moment my mother was pushing my sister and I in our pram down Otley Road to visit Auntie Hilda.

Is Auntie Hilda destined to take centre stage now? Her explanation of the Bettys mystery is quite simple. Around about 1915 there had been a London musical called 'Betty'! Frederick had seen the show and taken a real shine to its leading lady, called Betty. Auntie Hilda did not suggest that a relationship ensued; simply that is why a few years later he called his new venture 'Bettys'.

Betty Bronson

The play 'Betty' seemed to have sunk without trace: I could find no evidence of its existence, although I found a number of glamorous actresses of the period called Betty, including one – Betty Fairfax – whose publicity photos were taken by a photographer in Harrogate. Was she the elusive Betty who caught the rascally roving eye of my great-uncle?

The most famous celebrity baby of the time was also a Betty, and I have a dozen publicity postcards of 'Baby Betty', the daughter of the actors Ellaline Terriss and Seymour Hicks. She is cute, but surely not the face that launched a tea shop empire?

Two years later I tracked the play down at Bristol University's Theatre Collection. The more I learnt about the play, the more I realized why Frederick Belmont might have been drawn to this story of a humble servant girl who, through love, finds a place in society; a reflection of his own life story, perhaps?

Betty Blythe

Betty Balfour

Betty Fairfax

Little Betty Hicks

Daly's
Theatre
"Betty"

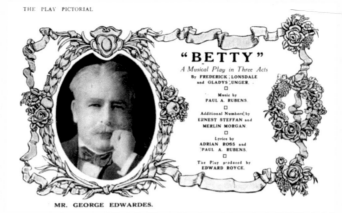

"BETTY"
A Musical Play in Three Acts
By FREDERICK LONSDALE
and GLADYS UNGER.

Music by
PAUL A. RUBENS.

Additional Numbers by
ERNEST STEFFAN and
MERLIN MORGAN

Lyrics by
ADRIAN ROSS and
PAUL A. RUBENS.

The Play produced by
EDWARD ROYCE.

MR. GEORGE EDWARDES.

I discovered that the impresario George Edwardes had put on 'Betty' at Daly's Theatre in London, first night 24th April, 1915. D. Forbes Wilmslow, the theatre historian, wrote:

'Cinderella is the oldest plot in musical comedy. "Find a new twist in it," stage people say, "and there is a fortune." In spite of innumerable adaptations made by so many authors, its sweet simplicity still finds interested audiences and sympathetic readers. Betty, a beautiful play set to charming music, exploits the sentiments of the Cinderella theme. It ran for 391 performances. A simpler or more tender little love piece was never produced at Daly's – that is the highest tribute I can pay to the charms of Betty.'

The twist in this tale is that this Cinderella is very badly treated by her prince. The Duke of Crowborough tells his wayward only son, Gerard, that he will disinherit him if he doesn't marry and settle down. In a fit of pique Gerard proposes to one of the kitchen maids, Betty, who accepts him and he tells her she must be ready to be married on the morrow. Next morning Gerard marries Betty, who carries herself like a princess; but still he rudely packs her off to the country and continues his wild bachelor life in London. The Duke is so incensed at his son's behaviour that he disinherits him and makes all his money over to Betty. After many more twists and turns *'the curtain drops on a very happy couple'.*

What makes Auntie Hilda's story all the more plausible was our discovery that the play came to Harrogate's Grand Opera House on no less than three occasions between 1916 and 1918. Was it just the story that attracted him, or was it one of the leading ladies? Did young Frederick Belmont fall for the charms of Miss Winifred Barnes, Miss Isobel Delorme, or Miss Nellie Taylor, all of whom starred as the young kitchen maid Betty?

MISS WINIFRED BARNES AS BETTY AND MASTER
CYRIL DOUGHTY AS A PERT PAGE

Betty Rose

Now the other story. In 1987 my father received a letter from two ladies who claimed that their aunt – still alive – had always told them that she was the Betty in 'Bettys'. Winifred Elizabeth Rose was her name, or simply Betty Rose. The nieces wrote that Betty Rose was the granddaughter of the lady who really founded Bettys, and that young Betty had walked into the dining room at her grandmother's house where the new directors were trying to decide what to call their café venture. Instead of telling her off for interrupting their meeting, grandmother looked at the lovely young Betty carrying a toy tea tray and decided: 'We will call it Bettys!'

I went to visit Betty Rose, then in her eighties and living in the Cotswolds. Unfortunately Betty could not recall the famous occasion itself, even though she would have been eleven or twelve at the time. It was her mother who always told her that Bettys was named after her following this chance interruption. Betty Rose was such a lovely lady, and so proud of her association, that I just had to adopt her as my official Betty. What clinched it was the hand-tinted old photograph of her on her dining-room wall: a portrait of a lovely little girl carrying a tea service.

It was long after Betty Rose's death that, with the help of her nieces and our company archives, I pieced together the background to the Betty Rose story.

In his letter of 21st February, 1921, Frederick Belmont alluded to other shareholders; *'but I am the only one that understands the business'.* What he didn't say was that the crucial funding had come from his new wife's Aunt Mary. Mary Wood was the widow of a very successful Harrogate grocer and tea dealer, John Wood. After his death in 1904 she continued to run the business in James Street herself. The Woods were staunch Quakers who were renowned for their philanthropy. Mary's generosity extended to her niece and her ambitious Swiss husband. It was Mary Wood who paid the deposit on the first premises and guaranteed the mortgage. She had certain conditions attached to her generosity, though. Her two sons were to be directors along with her son-in-law Frederick Rose, who was a baker. She herself would be chairman of the board.

So Frederick Belmont was just one director surrounded by a tightly knit group of in-laws. Not for long, though: Mary Wood died in 1925, and her sons lost interest and sold their shares to another investor, a Leeds wine merchant. It was another five years before Frederick and Claire, now Dickie and Bunny, bought all the shares for themselves.

Actually, it was a bit more scandalous than that. In fact one of Mary's sons, George Wood, a solicitor, ceased to be a director on being jailed for purloining clients' money.

However rascally her sons, I like the sound of Mary Wood. From a faded family photograph my father has painted her portrait for the board room at Bettys. I can see her chairing that first meeting in her dining room at home at what is now the Mile Post Inn on Leeds Road. I can see twelve-year-old Betty bringing in the tea. I can hear Mary Wood saying 'We'll call it Bettys'. Could it be true? Unfortunately all the evidence is circumstantial. Perhaps that's for the best.

Mary Wood

Bettys Tea Rooms were born of a love story – a romance between a young Swiss and his Harrogate landlady's daughter. It would be so appropriate if he had called the business after his bride.

Many of her friends and staff from that era believe she is Betty. Her name, however, is Claire, and the only familiar name by which she was known was 'Bunny', as can be testified by the ladies of Pannal Golf Club, who compete annually for the 'Bunny Belmont Trophy'. No, it cannot be her, unless... An old friend of hers, Jimmy Ogden, once told my father that in her youth Bunny was a beautician and hairdresser and that her professional name was Betty. Unfortunately, I cannot verify that. She had her own 'salon' in a room above a florist and all the advertisements for it are in her own name, 'Claire Appleton'. Another theory bites the dust?

The Bunny Belmont Trophy

Bunny Belmont

Actually, I quite like the thought that 'Bettys' could have been called 'Bunnys'! That would be infinitely preferable to 'Bettyfayre', a new name for Bettys proposed by some consultants in 1972.

Who can criticize us for staying loyal to Betty, whoever she may be.

The fact is that whenever my father asked his uncle 'Who was Betty?', Uncle changed the subject. *He did not want us to know.*

Going through the Wood and Rose family archives I came across an entry Mary Wood had made in her daughter's visitors' book on 9th April, 1897:

There is no happiness like that of being loved by your fellow creatures and feeling that your presence is an addition to their comfort.

Mary Wood

That would make a very good motto for Bettys. As an immigrant family the overwhelming desire always seemed to be not for riches but for acceptance and recognition by the community. Uncle truly relished being 'loved by his fellow creatures' and delighted in the thought that his creation – Bettys – was 'an addition to their comfort'.

What future generations will make of it all I do not know. The next book will have to be written by the fourth generation of the family. Maybe they will see more clearly. Not too clearly, I hope; there is something reassuring and comforting about myths and legends which can be spoiled by too much clarity. *He did not want us to know.*

If you have bought this book it must be because you know and love Bettys as a customer. Thank you. We will do our best to be around to serve your children and your children's children. I am sure they will still be asking the same old question: 'Just who was Betty?'

"Scuse me miss, are you Betty?'

Thank yous

This book would have remained unwritten were it not for my editor, Sarah McKee. She worked in Bettys shop in Ilkley for seven years, helping to pay her way through school, university, right through to her masters degree in history. She persuaded me to let her become our archivist for a year, and this book would not have been possible without her determination to put the company and family archives in good order. She has discovered photographs we didn't know we had, letters no one had got around to translating, and, above all, she charmed stories and anecdotes out of people renowned for their discretion and privacy.

Uncle always said: *'If we want something just right, we have to do it ourselves.'* True to his word we have designed and published this book ourselves. For over a year this has been a labour of love for our designer Georgina Gill. When she went on her maternity leave our head designer, Rebecca Watson, stepped in to complete the project. Appropriately the cover was designed by Georgina's maternity cover, Jane Jardine.

I would also like to give special thanks to:

Ruth Brock and Claire Cave, Bettys student archivists from 1998 to 2003, and Dawn Taylor, keeper of the keys from 1980 to the present.

My mother, Kay Wild, and my Swiss Aunt Hanni, for photographs and memories.

Rodney Light for the lovely photograph of his late wife, Valerie Belmont.

Shirley Penfold, Claire Taylor, Mary Hodgson, and Harold Clarke for Belmont mementoes and memories.

Ruth England and Jeanne Seagrove for photographs and memories of Betty Rose and Mary Wood.

The late Jim Raleigh, his late wife Muriel, and their godson Rixon Matthews, Helen Wrightson, Carole and Peter Topham, and the late Alison Taylor for photographs and memories of the Taylor family business.

The late Bill Baxter for entrusting us with Betty Lupton's cup and saucer.

The many staff who allowed us to 'snap' them at work.

The many retired staff who shared their memories of the old days.

The photographers who have captured the spirit (but not the ghost) of present-day Bettys: Tom Cutting, Graham Nelson, Nik Pikard, Tony Bartholomew, and Victor De Jesus. We took over 4,000 photographs to try and capture the atmosphere of Bettys. It was so difficult to choose which to use in this book, especially as so many customers were excited at the prospect of being included in this little piece of history. We are sorry to have disappointed so many.

For those who were caught on camera when they were supposed to be somewhere else, our sincere apologies. We endeavoured to get everyone's permission.

Every effort has been made to trace the copyright holders of additional material used in this book. We thank Eden Camp, Ian Boyle Shipping, Marine Art Posters, DND Canada, Graham Hall Postcards, Theatre Museum, Crispin Hughes/Oxfam, Don Burluraux, Christine Shepherd, the ILN Picture Library, Unnetie Digital Archive, and the NRM/SSPL who have all provided additional memorabilia and other images. If anyone has been overlooked, we will acknowledge them in any future editions.

The final dedication is to Victor Wild.
I am convinced he still has a few secrets up his sleeve,
but that's for another volume.

*My father, Victor Wild,
in his greenhouse with his
coffee and cocoa plants*

We hope you have enjoyed this book. If you would like further copies
please visit www.bettysandtaylors.co.uk or call in at one of our Bettys Café Tea Rooms:
Parliament Street, Harrogate
RHS Garden Harlow Carr, Harrogate
St Helen's Square, York
Stonegate, York
The Grove, Ilkley
High Street, Northallerton

If you think you know who Betty really is or have any anecdotes
or memorabilia for our archives, please write to me
at 1 Parliament Street, Harrogate HG1 2QU.
I look forward to hearing from you.